"God described David as a  _Tabernacle_ helps you and me a.... that moved the heart of God! This is one of the best books written on the subject! I highly recommend it!"

—Dr. Jason Hubbard, International Prayer Council

"I believe that the topic of David's Tabernacle and the centrality of God's presence is one of the most important and often neglected in the church today. I am so grateful for Matthew's leadership and for this book. The content of this book could be revolutionary for those that read it with an open heart and mind. I highly recommend it!"

—David Bradshaw, Founder of Awaken the Dawn

"I've known Matthew Lilley for years and I know first hand that he has devoted his life to studying, living, and leading others into this message. This book provides a much-needed theological bedrock for what God is doing in the earth through night-and-day worship and prayer. It's one of the best-researched works on David's Tabernacle I've ever read. It will stir you, challenge you and provoke you to join the great prayer movement sweeping the earth."

—David Fritch, Author of _Enthroned: Bringing God's Kingdom to Earth Through Unceasing Worship & Prayer_

"I believe we are in a season where the Holy Spirit is highlighting the Tabernacle of David to the Body of Christ as the blueprint for the next generation of pioneering leaders to build presence-centered communities. The end of the story is that every nation will see the worth of Jesus and every nation will sing. This is a must read for any one who desires to be right at the center of what God is doing across the earth right now in preparation for the return of His Son, the son of David. The intertwining of theology, personal experience, and prophetic insight will make *David's Tabernacle* an enjoyable read for everyone. Matthew masterfully lays out the biblical narrative for this long forgotten piece of God's redemptive plan for the nations and my prayer is that everyone who reads this book will find their place in God's story as He rebuilds the fallen Tabernacle of David across the earth."

—R.A. Martinez, President, MAPS GLOBAL

"I've given my entire adult life to see the resting place of God's presence take hold in the church, cities, and nations. My life prayer has been as King David said 'I will not give sleep to my eyes or slumber to my eyelids, until I find a place for the Lord...' In a culture full of echoes and copies, authentic and unique voices become all the more necessary. Matthew Lilley is such a voice, for such a time as this. The groundwork laid in this book will become the foundation for what I believe is crashing into the earth in this moment of history: the rebuilding of David's Tabernacle. This will usher in the greatest harvest of souls in all of human history. It will transform entire cities and it will beautify the bride in her first love pursuit. Matthew and his revelation and understanding of the Tabernacle of David and the worship and prayer movement are hard to find; this subject is integral to the church and yet it is so hard to find substantial, biblical, and simplified teaching on it. His writings have inspired me that indeed God's dream to build a resting place in the earth through His priesthood is alive and well!"

—Chris Burns, Worship Leader and Revivalist

"Few things touch the heart of God like worship. The depths of this topic have been explored by many, but none have dug as deeply into the life and practice of David. Matthew unpacks his personal journey and years of experience to help us understand the power that is available to the houses of worship we steward. I cannot encourage you enough to read this book and apply its practice to your life and the ministry you oversee. Simply put, some things are set apart and holy unto God, and worship is one of those. If we are to welcome His presence and host His Spirit, we must recognize what He responds to. Preference cannot guide our worship; only His voice and the application of His Word can take us where the depths of our spirit want to go."

—AARON KENNEDY, Lead Pastor, Opendoor Church
(North Carolina)

"*David's Tabernacle* is a much needed book in an hour that the Church desperately needs answers. The old way of doing church will not sustain us through the challenges of the days ahead, and Matthew Lilley gives us a clear perspective on how the Church can stand with the Lord's presence and power in this most important time. Matthew's own journey of how the Lord met him as a youth, intertwined with the details of David's Tabernacle, give us a helpful and insightful roadmap as to how the Lord can cause us to have a heart like David. Through these pages Matthew offers historical precedent as well as prophetic perspective on how the Lord is releasing ministry in the spirit of the Tabernacle of David in our day. I encourage you to read with a heart open and expectant as to what the Spirit is saying to the Church. I believe Matthew has captured the heart of the Lord for this hour and the days ahead."

—BILLY HUMPHREY, Director, GateCity Church

THE TAB

COLLECTIVE

GET THE FULL EXPERIENCE:
JOIN THE TAB COLLECTIVE!

The Tab Collective is an exclusive online community that believes that God's presence changes everything.

Before you start reading the book, sign up to receive:

- Access to a private Facebook group to discuss the book content and all things related to worship, prayer, mission and the kingdom of God

- Exclusive access to addendums to the book including articles such as "Hindrances to Evangelical Interest in David's Tabernacle" and "The Convergence of 24-7 Prayer and David's Tabernacle in the 20th Century"

- Special access and/or discounts to future webinars, panels and conferences on themes related to David's tabernacle

- Early access & discounts on future books, products and merchandise from Matthew Lilley and Presence Pioneers

You can learn more at http://collective.davidstabernacle.com.

Scan this QR code using your phone's camera to sign up now!

DAVID'S TABERNACLE

HOW GOD'S PRESENCE CHANGES EVERYTHING

Matthew Lilley

Inscribe Press
Creativity Unleashed

DAVID'S TABERNACLE
How God's presence changes everything

Published by Inscribe Press, Fredericksburg, VA
Cover design by Kinsey Schick.
(https://kinseykateschick.myportfolio.com/work)

ISBN   978-1-951611-22-4 Print
       978-1-951611-23-1 eBook

Contents

Acknowledgements

To my wife and parents—I am deeply grateful for your encouragement over the years to write a book. I finally did it.

To Jeffrey Pelton and Kinsey Schick—thank you for all your hard work in seeing this book become a finished product. To the book launch team—thank you for praying this project through the finish line and celebrating the release with me.

To those who have supported me in pursuing this Davidic calling—there are way too many ministry partners, pastors, mentors, friends and colleagues to name; thank you for helping me experience the power of God's presence and therefore giving me something to write about.

To those who have gone before me in this journey of studying and living out the heart of David's tabernacle—thank you for laying the foundation upon which this book rests. I quote most of you somewhere in these pages.

To my children and those who will go after me—may this book be a resource for your generation to experience more of God's glorious presence and kingdom.

Preface

Despite growing up in church, I did not hear anything about David's tabernacle until I was in my late teens or early twenties. I knew that David wrote songs. I knew he was king of Israel. I knew he had some trouble with Bathsheba. I knew that there was an "Old Testament tabernacle" originally built by Moses. I had even attended Bible studies where we looked at the symbolic significance of the furniture, sacrifices, and rituals of Moses's tabernacle. I knew that there was eventually a permanent Temple built in Jerusalem for Israel. But I didn't realize there was a third tabernacle. Sandwiched between the tabernacle built by Moses and the Temple built by Solomon was a tent of worship established by David.

David's tabernacle is strikingly unique in the biblical narrative. As we will discover, King David established Israel's capital in Jerusalem and set up the worship tent there on Mt Zion. He placed the Ark of the Covenant (the place of God's presence) in the tent, which was accessible for all of the Levites—and even David himself—at any time. He appointed musicians and singers to stand before God and sing prayers, prophesy, and praise day and night for the entire thirty-three years of his reign in Jerusalem. Many of the Psalms were likely written in this tent, including some of the most notable messianic prophecies in the Old Testament.

The powerful atmosphere of worship brought great blessing on David and the nation during this era.

The tabernacle of David[1] is a powerful foreshadowing of the Church of Jesus Christ, and it has profound implications for us as Christians. It impacts the three "directions" of our primary relationships: up (how we relate to God), in (how we relate to other Christians), and out (how we relate to the lost).[2] Insights regarding these practical implications are scattered throughout this book.

A Neglected Story

When the Lord began drawing me into the study of David's tabernacle over fifteen years ago, I was blown away by the limited number of resources available on this subject. I felt a supernatural urge to understand what David had done and the implications of it in my life, but I felt like maybe I was a little crazy. Why were so few people talking about this? Why was there so little commentary? Why so few books? Why was David's tabernacle being overlooked? Every time I explored the topic, I felt like I was touching something so near to God's heart, and over the years, it has become near to my heart, too.

I soon found out that I was not alone in my challenges in finding materials on David's tabernacle. Bible scholar Peter Leithart says, "Christians have devoted much effort to understanding the

---

1   As you may already notice, I use the terms "David's tabernacle," "tabernacle of David," "tent of David," and "David's tent" interchangeably to describe the same thing: the tent of worship established by David in Jerusalem.

2   In theological terms, we could say that David's tabernacle speaks to our doxology (up), ecclesiology (in) and missiology (out). I believe David's tabernacle also impacts our eschatology—the study of the end times—although I am much less confident in that area of study. This book only touches eschatology in a minor way towards the later chapters.

typological and theological significance of the Mosaic tabernacle and the temple of Solomon, but comparatively little effort has been expended on the study of the liturgical situation in the time of David or its implications for Christian worship. The scholarly literature is relatively sparse. Commentators on Samuel and Chronicles of course mention David's tent and the worship performed there, but few articles and monographs have attempted to study it in detail."[3]

Methodist minister George Smith wrote about the tabernacle of David in the mid-19th century: "It is scarcely possible to find a more neglected, or a more important, portion of scriptural inquiry than this."[4] Kevin Conner wrote one of the most influential books on the topic in the 1970s, yet when he first heard the phrase "tabernacle of David" he admits, "I did not even know that David had a tabernacle."[5]

Another Book on David's Tabernacle

There are thousands of Christian books on prayer, marriage, the end times and many other topics. However, very few people are talking about David's tabernacle, and anything I can do to bring awareness of these truths to a few more believers is a success for me. If nothing else, I hope this book helps a handful of people realize that David did have a tabernacle, and it matters. A lot.

Over the years I have done my best to find any books, articles, videos, or teachings that discuss this rather neglected biblical theme. For this book, I have pulled together stories, teachings,

---

3   Peter Leithart, *From Silence to Song: The Liturgic Davidic Revolution* (Moscow, ID: Canon Press, 2003), 13.

4   *The Harmony of the Divine Dispensations,* 149.

5   Kevin Conner, *The Tabernacle of David* (Portland, OR: City Bible Publishing, 1976), ii.

and concepts from several sources, including some that are out of print or relatively obscure. Most of all, I've spent countless hours studying and praying through the relevant Scripture passages. This book serves primarily as a Bible teaching.

Where does this book fit in with the others that are already published about the tabernacle of David? Some existing writings are scholarly and academic, and therefore their material is rather challenging for the general public to digest. They also tend to lack the prophetic perspective of a Spirit-filled author. Some charismatic authors have already written some user-friendly material which is more accessible than the scholarly writings. However, much of the charismatic literature does not dive deeply into key biblical passages and themes I have discovered in my study. My goal is to provide a book on David's tabernacle that is deep but accessible. I try to avoid too many theological terms or original languages, but I also take the time to provide a rather in-depth Bible study. This was written for hungry worshipers of Jesus who want to go deep with God and enter more fully into all He is doing on the earth.

Along with curating content from multiple unique sources, most notably the Bible, I share how my personal story and ministry experience have aligned with the truths found in the story of David's tabernacle. This is not just a book of theory and theology, but a book birthed from the experience of trying to live and minister with the "spirit" of the tabernacle of David. The premise of this book is that God's presence changes everything. My personal story with the Lord, and many stories of my ministry experience, testify to this very truth.

In this book I also attempt to approach David's tabernacle from a unique angle compared to other works. Many writers begin their discussion with the verses about the restoration of David's tabernacle from Amos 9:11 and Acts 15:16-17. Instead, I spend more time on what exactly happened in David's original worship tent and what inspired his unique expressions of worship. It is not until much later in the book that I begin to approach the prophetic passages about the rebuilding of the tabernacle of David.

Do We Really Understand David's Tabernacle?

Despite years of deep interest in David's tabernacle, I still have the sense that my understanding of this wonderful subject is limited. Every time I explore these related Scripture passages, I find myself making new discoveries and receiving fresh revelation. I am continually realizing how pervasive the influence of David's worship and kingdom are to the entire biblical storyline. In this book, I do my best to lay out the grandeur of the topic, but I realize that I will inevitably fall short in articulating all that could be written on the matter.[6] The sense of entering a vast ocean of uncharted water seems to be common with those who have taken time to dive into deep study of David's tabernacle.

Peter Leithart, whom I quote extensively, is one of my favorite authors on the topic—not because I agree 100% with all of his answers, but because he is one of the few Bible teachers that I found who was even asking some of the same questions. He said as he has studied David's tabernacle that "It is still getting bigger, and I still feel that the peak is a ways ahead, somewhere up there through the fog."[7] I can relate.

An acquaintance of mine, who has led prayer ministries inspired by David's tabernacle for years, began to be led by the Lord

---

6   I may need to release revised editions or follow-up books in the coming years. This sense of having such an incomplete grasp on the subject was part of why I was hesitant to write this book. Yet I felt prompted by the Lord—and by strong urgings from my wife along with a few prophetic words—that I needed to move ahead. I trust it will be a helpful addition to the limited library of writings on this subject.

7   Leithart, *From Silence to Song*, 7.

to study this subject again in early 2020. He says God spoke to him boldly that "You don't know anything about the tabernacle of David, and hardly anyone does." If this is true, the implications are stunning.

David Schoch, who released a prophetic word in the 1960s that led to a wave of initial interest in David's tabernacle in the charismatic movement, said in 2001, "I don't believe we're through with all that God wants to speak about David's tabernacle, yet. We've only touched a part of it."[8] After nearly four decades of teachings, study, books and practice around the theme of Davidic worship, he was convinced that "we've only touched part of it."

My hope is that this book touches another part of it.

---

8   Quoted from a transcript of an interview that I received from Vivian Hibbert.

One Thing is Needed

One thing I have desired of the Lord, that will I seek: That I may dwell in the house of the Lord all the days of my life, to behold the beauty of the Lord, and to inquire in His temple (Psalm 27:4).

One night, in the summer of 2002, I lay for hours on the stinky floor of a Christian youth camp in eastern North Carolina, and had an encounter with God that changed the trajectory of my life.

I had arrived at camp confused and disillusioned. Like many young adults that age, I was wrestling with what to do with my life. My identity, my future vocation, and my college plans were in limbo.

Just six months earlier, I had it all figured out. I was dating a popular girl at school. My friends and I had started a popular band that was covering 90s grunge songs and writing a few of our own. We even won the local battle of the bands at the largest concert venue in downtown Greenville, NC. I was taking classical guitar lessons so that I could major in music at East Carolina University. I needed the degree as a backup plan, but my real ambition was to be a famous rock star. I was on track to be cool and successful.

By the time I graduated high school, my girlfriend had dumped me. The cool rock band had disbanded, as some of the musicians were going off to college. My guitar teacher had moved away and left me unprepared to audition for the music school at ECU. I was confused and rethinking my life goals. That is when I arrived at summer camp.

The Holy Spirit was moving powerfully at this youth camp. Many students were experiencing the power of the Holy Spirit through salvation, healing, and deliverance. It was common to have students on their knees weeping or knocked to the floor by God's power. Individuals would be so "drunk" from the power of the Holy Spirit that counselors had to carry them back to their bunk beds (Acts 2:15, Ephesians 5:18). This was the kind of charismatic church camp experience in which I was immersed.

Four days into the week, I found myself frustrated. I was not experiencing God's presence and power like many other kids. I wondered if they were faking it. I hadn't cried or gotten knocked over by God's power. I didn't feel inebriated. And I was not about to fake it. Yeah, I liked some of the music. I felt a mild sense of God's love for me. The counselors were kind. They prayed with me and talked to me. They were even honest and said some kids probably faked it. They assured me that everyone experiences the Holy Spirit differently, and some people react more strongly to it than others.

On one of the last nights of camp, there was an extended time of musical worship after the message. Counselors made their way around the room to lay hands on the students and pray for them. When my fellow campers began experiencing God's power again, I decided to lie on the floor. I didn't know what else to do. I was not feeling God, so I just gave up.

What started in frustration ended in glory. God met me on

that pungent floor. I lay there for hours with my eyes closed. God began to speak to me, reveal His love to me, and describe His purposes for my life. I had a vision of Jesus inviting me into His lap to experience His love. His perfect love set me free from the fear and insecurity (I John 4:18) that had dominated my teenage years.

There were a few intriguing supernatural moments to this encounter. I distinctly recall lying on the smelly camp floors. Yet after God met me there, I distinctly smelled aroma of perfumes. This stuck out to me because I had noted how badly the floor smelled when I first lay down! I later found out that throughout the Bible God describes sacrifices offered to Him as a "pleasing aroma."[1]

The experience also included supernatural sounds. While lying there, I heard a beautiful female voice singing a specific worship song—a song we sang often at our youth group. I could tell it was someone near me in the room. When I got off the floor hours later, I asked around to find out who was singing that song. It turns out it was Katie from our youth group. Katie was notorious for being a poor singer! She always sang boldly, loudly, and extremely off key. Yet I heard a beautiful voice that night. God let me hear worship the way He hears it. God let me hear the song of her heart, which was beautiful to Him.

I also saw visions of myself leading worship. God told me that my gifts and music were to be used for His glory, not my own. He said I was to be like King David who carried God's presence into his city. He said I was to be an "undignified" worshiper who was free from fear and passionate for God. Even in these supernatural encounters, God was teaching me what was important to Him and inviting me into His purposes for my life.

---

1   Genesis 8:21, Exodus 29:18, Leviticus 17:6, etc.

At that moment I said *yes*. Yes to receiving His love. Yes to being a worshiper. And yes to being like King David.

I later reflected on that summer camp encounter as a moment of offering myself to God as a "living sacrifice," which the Bible calls our "spiritual worship" (Romans 12:1). This encounter was a major step along the journey of God, bringing me into an understanding of David's tabernacle. At that time, I did not realize the significance of the seeds God was planting in my heart. Yet I came home with the realization of the power of God's presence in extended times of worship and prayer. I was aware of the "camp high" that tended to fade after a few weeks; I didn't want my experience to end. I wondered if it was truly possible for my friends and I to stay "on fire" for God for years to come. Maybe if we could recreate that camp environment at our home church, we could sustain our passion and even help others encounter God's presence in the life-changing way that I had.

The Heart of David

I began this book with my personal journey, not only because it exemplifies the message of this book—that God's presence changes everything—but also because the story of David's tabernacle begins with David. Without David's heart and life, you never get his kingdom and tabernacle. Before David offered the wealth of a nation to establish day and night praise and worship at the tent in Jerusalem, he offered his heart before God on the hillsides while watching the sheep for his father.

David was the only person in the Bible called a man after God's own heart (I Samuel 13:14, Acts 13:22). Without the heart and zeal of David, there is no tabernacle of David. His uniquely intimate and personal relationship with the Lord set the stage for the nation of Israel to be brought into that same nearness to

Be you (in the prayer rooms)
don't be
anyone else.

God's glory and presence.

The book of 1 Chronicles gives us insight into the story and structure of the tabernacle of David, but the Psalms give us insight into the *heart* of the tabernacle of David. Some believe that many of the psalms from David and Asaph were written in David's tent at Zion. Perhaps they were spontaneous "new" songs that were written by the scribes there.

A glance at these songs illuminates the obsession with the presence of God at David's tabernacle.

As a deer pants for flowing streams, so pants my soul for you, O God. My soul thirsts for God, for the living God. When shall I come and appear before God? (Psalm 42:1-2).

How lovely is your dwelling place, O Lord of hosts! My soul longs, yes, faints for the courts of the Lord; my heart and flesh sing for joy to the living God. For a day in your courts is better than a thousand elsewhere. I would rather be a doorkeeper in the house of my God than dwell in the tents of wickedness (Psalm 84:1-2, 10).

The One Thing

The pursuit of God's presence was the driving force of David's life. He articulated this deep longing by saying that there was "one thing" that he desired. He longed to be in the place of worship, gazing upon God's beauty, hearing His voice and dwelling in His presence forever.

David the outcast craved the temple

One thing I have desired of the LORD, that will I seek: That I may dwell in the house of the LORD all the days of my life, to behold the beauty of the LORD, and to inquire in His temple (Psalm 27:4).

Obviously David wanted more than one thing, and gave his

13

attention to more than one thing. He was also a king and military leader with many natural responsibilities. Yet there was one overarching desire in his heart that eclipsed all other desires. He longed for communion with God. David's cry for "one thing" was for the prioritization of His relationship with God above everything else.

David knew that if he got this one thing right, it would bring blessing and fruitfulness to everything he puts his hands to. Likewise, if he got this one thing wrong, it would ripple negatively into every other area of his life, work, and ministry. He understood that all prosperity, joy, and victory was an overflow from God's presence with him. This heart posture would set the tone for all of David's reign as king and lead to the establishment of David's tabernacle; but it had to be personal first. The other notable time we see the exact phrase "one thing" in Scriptures is the story of Mary of Bethany in the New Testament. Here we find another extravagant worshiper!

> Now it happened as they went that He entered a certain village; and a certain woman named Martha welcomed Him into her house. And she had a sister called Mary, who also sat at Jesus' feet and heard His word. But Martha was distracted with much serving, and she approached Him and said, "Lord, do You not care that my sister has left me to serve alone? Therefore tell her to help me." And Jesus answered and said to her, "Martha, Martha, you are worried and troubled about many things. But <u>one thing is needed</u>, and Mary has chosen that good part, which will not be taken away from her" (Luke 10:38-42).

Amid all that was going on, Mary sat at the feet of Jesus to hear His voice and experience His presence. Jesus told Martha that what Mary was doing was the "one thing" that was needed.

Jesus commended the way Mary prioritized her relationship *with* Him over doing things *for* Him. I think it is likely that Jesus is using the phrase "one thing" to describe Mary in order to hint back to David's extravagant worship in Psalm 27:4.

The Desire of God

What was the source of David's zeal and passion for God's presence? It was not his personality. It was not brute determination. What was fueling his desire for the one thing?

David was connecting to an external source that was empowering his pursuit of the Lord. David's zeal was the zeal of Jesus. This truth becomes evident when you look at Jesus' high priestly prayer in John 17. This passage is the longest recorded prayer of Jesus in the Bible, and it gives us some amazing insight into the heart of God. Let's zero in on verse 24.

Father, I desire that they also, whom you have given me, may be with me where I am, to see my glory that you have given me because you loved me before the foundation of the world (John 17:24).

Jesus's prayer to the Father here is a fervent cry to have His people near Him in intimate relationship. You can feel the deep love of Jesus for us. He desires to bring us into that eternal flame of love that flows between the Father, Son, and Holy Spirit within the Godhead. Jesus was yearning to have His people close to Him to experience the fullness of His passionate love.

David tapped into this desire of Jesus and reciprocated that desire to God. The parallels between John 17:24 and Psalm 27:4 are uncanny.

David prayed "One thing I have desired" and Jesus prayed "Father I desire."

David prayed "That I may dwell in the house of the Lord," and Jesus prayed "that they also whom You gave Me may be with Me where I am."

David prayed "To behold the beauty of the Lord," and Jesus prayed "that they may behold My glory."

Long before Jesus walked the earth, David was articulating the same phrases that would be prayed by the Son of God. The longings of David's heart had aligned with the Lord. This is why he was a man after God's own heart—because the "one thing" David wanted was the same thing Jesus wanted. Likewise, as we walk in intimacy with the Lord, we will find our hearts in agreement to the yearnings of God's heart. The truth is, the only reason we can love and desire Him is because He first loved and desired us (I John 4:19). It is His longing for us that fuels our longing for an intimate relationship with Him.

The Secret Place

When I got home from my summer camp encounter in 2002, I was eager for others to taste the same presence and power that I had experienced in extended hours of worship at camp. This would be the impetus for me to launch into ministry. More importantly, I began pursuing God in a personal and private way at home. I found a Bible reading plan to help me read through the whole Bible in a year. I started worshiping God with my guitar in my room. I started journaling; pouring out my messy, young-adult thoughts and feelings to God. Sometimes I would even have ideas, thoughts, words, and phrases pop into my mind. I wrote those down too. I realized I was starting to hear God's voice.

Many times I would play worship music and lie on the floor for hours, basking in God's presence and receiving God's love for me, just like I had done at camp. I later learned that some people called this "soaking" in God's presence. Initially, I would not have called most of this activity "prayer." I thought prayer was boring. I liked "worship" because I equated it with music. But the truth is, I *was* learning to enjoy prayer. I was cultivating intimacy with God. Though it was messy and I was young, I was developing a deep and real relationship with a living God in what Jesus called the "secret place."

> *And when you pray, you shall not be like the hypocrites. For they love to pray standing in the synagogues and on the corners of the streets, that they may be seen by men. Assuredly, I say to you, they have their reward. But you, when you pray, go into your room, and when you have shut your door, <u>pray to your Father who is in the secret place;</u> and your Father who sees in secret will reward you openly. (Matthew 6:5-6, NKJV)*

Jesus promises that the Father will reward you if you pursue Him in secret. David learned this "secret place" principle early in his life. He knew he could fight Goliath in public because he had fought the lion and the bear in private. He could play his harp before King Saul and demons would flee, because he had learned to move God's heart with his songs on the hillsides as he watched sheep. This core value of intimacy with God was crucial to David's success. It's undoubtedly part of why God calls him a man after His own heart. It is vital to understand that the seed for David's tabernacle was planted and watered in David's secret place with God.

Laid-Down Lovers

It is in the hidden places of obscurity that God prepares vessels for His plan. It's in the place of intimacy with the Lord that God confronts pride, idolatry, and self-sufficiency. It's in the weakness of prayer that God endues His people with power. Those who have fallen in love with God become what Heidi Baker calls "laid down lovers" who are abandoned to God's purposes.

I've heard it said that "lovers outwork workers." In other words, people motivated to work out of duty will wear out faster than those who are motivated to work out of delight. It's amazing what love will do to motivate the human heart. Love for God marked David's life. His name means "beloved." From the overflow of love he would give his life to see God's dream for his generation.

For David, after he had served the purpose of God in his own generation, fell asleep and was laid with his fathers (Acts 13:36).

The revelation of David's tabernacle is powerful and expansive. As we will see, it involves the transformation of cities and nations. It is related to the kingdom of God coming to the earth. It is part of God's end-time strategy to finish the Great Commission. But the heart of it all is God's desire for intimacy with His people. That revelation of intimacy with God is at the core of David's story.

Don't miss this. Pursue God. Get in the secret place. Pray. Dive into Scripture. Worship when no one is looking. Get lost in the presence of God in your home. David's tabernacle is an epic story of God's redemption for all humanity, but it all begins with *one thing.*

Enthroned in Praise

The Power of God's Presence

I returned home from my summer camp experience with fire in my heart for others to experience God's presence the way I did. My encounter with God had occurred during an extended time of intimate, musical worship at camp, so I figured the game plan for revival should be to recreate that environment when we got back to our home church.

Inspired by the story of King David, I launched a Friday night youth worship night called "6:22." I had recently discovered a worship song titled "Undignified," and I realized it was based on the story of David in 2 Samuel 6, where he danced wildly through the street as the ark of the covenant was making its procession into Jerusalem. In the face of criticism for his wild praise, King David responded in verse 22 with what became the lyrics to the chorus: "I will become even more undignified than this." This song "Undignified" would become our theme song, and the ministry was named after that verse.

Every Friday night we would gather for two or three hours of non-stop, wild worship with around a hundred teenagers from churches all over our area. We would push the chairs to the side of the room so people had space to dance. We would crank up the volume and sing our hearts out to God. This is what made sense to do. I was no longer going to play music for myself. So I put together a band that would "jam" for God. Our core motivation was to help others experience the presence of God that I experienced at camp and in the secret place. From its very roots our ministry carried the "spirit" of the tabernacle of David. It was always about extravagant musical worship and helping people experience God's life-changing presence.

The Holy Spirit began moving powerfully at these 6:22 meetings. We soon discovered that when we praise and worship God the way the Bible describes, with our hearts truly engaged, God's presence manifested in powerful ways. When we first launched, we decided to look up "praise" in the Bible and simply do what it said to do. We discovered that the book of Psalms and a few New Testament verses gave us the clearest instruction. At the beginning of our Friday night gatherings, I would read the lists of "praise" passages from the Psalms, and then we would just try it! In faith and obedience we would sing, play our instruments, lift our hands, dance, bow down, and pray. We would even try to "sing a new song" by spending time in spontaneous worship between the pre-written songs.

As we worshiped, God touched students in tangible ways. Many would weep, cry, shake, laugh, and experience deep repentance and freedom. Salvation and physical healing began to manifest. We found that the demons that tormented our friends could not stand to be in the presence of God. Some of our fellow teenagers would either get set free or literally flee from the property! Light and darkness could not inhabit the same space.

One night, a young girl crossed the threshold of the main

worship room and immediately spun around, vomiting on the floor. (This can be a sign of demonic possession.) The leadership team quickly surrounded her and helped her into the kitchen for prayer. We found that our kitchen was regularly becoming our makeshift deliverance room. I recall a young man rolling his head around along the side wall, with the evil spirits inside of him enraged by the glory of God he was experiencing. We were quickly and dramatically discovering the power of God's presence.

Praise As An Invitation to Encounter

I had experienced this very phenomenon in my summer camp encounter. Musical "praise" seemed to create an environment where the Spirit of God met people in transformative ways. C.S. Lewis discovered this same principle while reflecting on the Psalms. He was curious about God's numerous commands for people to give Him praise. Why would a God without any needs demand people honor Him with their words? God is not insecure and in need of affirmation. God is not arrogant. Lewis received the revelation that praise and worship are God's means of allowing people to experience His presence. In his 1958 book *Reflections on the Psalms* he wrote:

> It is in the process of being worshipped that God communi-cates His presence to men. It is not of course the only way. But for many people at many times the "fair beauty of the Lord" is revealed chiefly or only while they worship Him together. [1]

Lewis realized that if praise and worship is a primary way in which we experience God's tangible presence, it means that God's command that we praise Him is actually an invitation into encounter with Him! It is God's love and yearning that urges His

---

1   C.S. Lewis, "A Word about Praising," chap. 9 in *Reflections on the Psalms* (Edison, NJ: First Inspirational Press, 1994).

people to sing. This is why David wrote in Psalm 100 that we "come before his presence with singing" and "enter his courts with praise."

God's invitation to the Church is to worship the way David worshiped—to embrace the same heart posture of love and devotion to God, but also to embrace the same biblical expressions of praise found throughout the Bible—especially in the book of Psalms. These include things like singing,[2] playing musical instruments,[3] shouting/cheering/clapping,[4] lifting our hands,[5] dancing and rejoicing,[6] and bowing down before the Lord.[7] These were the expressions of the praise and worship at David's tabernacle.

Throughout church history, the book of Psalms has been used for Christian worship. Some people try to reject fresh emphasis on Davidic worship as a modern invention without precedent in church history and tradition. However, the songbook of David's tent has been the songbook of the Christian church for the last two millennia. Believers throughout history have been reading, praying, and singing the same lyrics that were sung in that historic worship tent in Jerusalem.

While in-depth teaching on David's tabernacle has been scarce, Davidic worship has not . Even if the teaching and language of David's tabernacle is not used, the spirit of the tabernacle of David has been alive and well throughout church history. Christians have always been singers and worshipers, and the book of Psalms has held a unique place of value in all Christian worship traditions.

---

2 In the ESV, the book of Psalms alone uses the word "sing" 67 times and "song" 59 times!

3 Psalm 150.

4 Psalm 32:11, 47:1-5, 95:11

5 Psalm 28:2, 63:4, 134:2, 141:2

6 Psalm 149:3

7 Psalm 95:6

Hundreds of years before C.S. Lewis, while studying David's musicians in the writings of I Chronicles, the famous composer J.S. Bach wrote, "In devotional music, God is always present with His grace."[8] I imagine that the Scripture passages that Bach was reading confirmed what he had already experienced while writing and performing music for the Lord.

My friends and I discovered the power of praise at summer camp. J.S. Bach came to that understanding while reading about David's tabernacle in I Chronicles. For C.S. Lewis, it was the book of Psalms that helped open his eyes to God's purposes for worship. Other notable figures came to this realization in more dramatic ways.

Rediscovering the Psalm 22:3 Key

The idea that we experience God's presence through musical praise and worship is now commonplace in the body of Christ. It seems almost silly to mention it. But this was not always the case. This biblical idea that God's presence comes as we praise and worship Him has been rediscovered by the Church in the twentieth and twenty-first centuries. Modern worship historians have traced the proliferation of this truth to a relatively unknown pastor named Reg Layzell.[9]

Reg Layzell was a Canadian layman who reluctantly became a pastor during the Latter Rain revival of the 1940s and 50s. In 1946, he was invited as a guest preacher at a church where the pastor became ill. Layzell was required to single-handedly lead a

---

8   John W. Kleinig, *The Lord's Song* (Sheffield, England: Sheffield Academic Press, 1993), 13.

9   I want to thank Dr. Lester Ruth and his research team at Duke Divinity School for making me aware of Reg Layzell and the importance of the Latter Rain revival in the modern development of praise and worship. Ruth's book Loving' on Jesus provides a concise history of contemporary worship for those who are interested in learning more.

week of special services that had been scheduled, and he initially struggled. He recalls:

"I stumbled and perspired my way through the morning service. I was embarrassed, and I'm sure the people were not at all impressed with the great evangelist. The meeting Sunday night was rather ordinary and I was thankful when it was all over." [10]

After a few nights of bad meetings, he was desperately crying out to God for help. That Wednesday, during a time of prayer, the verse Psalm 22:3 came to his mind. In the King James Bible, he read:

But thou art holy, O thou that inhabitest the praises of Israel. [11]

His initial thought was that God wanted to emphasize holiness. But while focusing on God's holiness in prayer, the entire verse continued to ring out in his mind. Then he noticed the word "praise," so he began to praise the Lord. The Holy Spirit brought various Psalms to his mind about praising God with singing, clapping, and bowing. As Pastor Layzell praised the Lord, God's presence flooded the church building. He spent hours that afternoon walking around speaking and singing praises. He realized God was teaching him how He "dwells" in praises. Layzell praised until the evening service began. Here is what happened next:

"Then the meeting started and I announced the hymn 'There is Power in the Blood.' I will always remember that. We sang

---

10   Reginald Layzell, *Pastor's Pen: Firsthand Accounts of the 1948 Prophetic Revival* (Independently published, 2019), 163-164.

11   Certain translations of Psalm 22:3 say that God "inhabits" praise and some translations say that God is "enthroned" in praise.

the first verse, the second verse, and then the chorus. Suddenly a girl on one side of the church threw her hands up and began to speak in tongues. About 5 minutes later a sister on the other side began to shout and speak in tongues—then someone in the center aisle. They were baptized in the Holy Spirit!... Thus was born the message of praise, which is the secret of continuous revival. He lives in the praises of his people!"[12]

While God was moving at the service, the pastor who was home sick was supernaturally healed in his bed while they worshiped at the church building![13] God was teaching this pastor the reality of God's presence amid those who praise and worship Him as the Psalms describe.

Reg Layzell befriended the early leaders of the Latter Rain revival,[14] and his teachings on praise spread virally as that movement grew across the world in the mid-twentieth century. His conviction was that praise sustained the revival. "The foundation of the visitation, as expressed in these churches, is praise and worship... the sacrifice of praise brought with it continuous revival" (pg 153). This "continuous revival" included seasons of twenty-four-hour prayer in some of the Latter Rain-influenced churches in the late 1940s.[15]

Layzell's teaching on praise and worship emphasized the New Testament command to offer a "sacrifice of praise" (Hebrews 13:15) in addition to his initial revelation from Psalm 22:3. In contrast to the popular Pentecostal teachings that believers should "tarry" for God's presence to come upon you, the Latter Rain

---

12   Layzell, *Pastor's Pen*, 165.

13   Layzell, *Pastor's Pen*, xiv.

14   The Latter Rain revival started in Canada in the late 1940s and grew into a broader movement that would be profoundly influential in pentecostal-charismatic history.

15   Layzell, *Pastor's Pen*, xvii.

revival (due to Layzell's influence) taught that you could simply praise God of your own volition and experience God's manifest presence at any time.

"Feelings or not, I will praise you! I will give You the fruit of my lips. Here it comes. Glory to God. I don't feel like it. I don't want to do it, but it is what You asked for, and You can have it. Hallelujah!"[16]

One way that Layzell taught this principle is by inviting everyone forward after his sermon. He would pull out his watch and ask people to praise God for ten minutes. Reluctantly, people would slowly force themselves to speak and sing praises to God, beginning to cry out "Hallelujah!" "Bless you Lord!" "We honor you!" Within a few minutes, God's presence was palpable among the people. Yet after the ten minutes were up, Layzell would ask everyone to halt and then end the meeting. Of course, no one wanted to stop, once they were experiencing God's glory, but the point had been made.[17]

God used people like Reg Layzell and C.S. Lewis to bring the biblical truth about "praise" back to the forefront of the Church's theology and practice in the twentieth century. The body of Christ began to rediscover what Bach recognized hundreds of years ago and King David realized thousands of years before that—that God is enthroned in the praise of His people.

---

16   Layzell, *Pastor's Pen*, 158.

17   This story was shared with me during an interview with Lester Ruth, which can be accessed at http://www.presencepioneers.org/38/

Sing a New Song

Oh sing to the Lord a new song; sing to the Lord, all the earth!
(Psalm 96:1)

Like Reg Layzell, David would discover the power of praise through a series of supernatural experiences with Samuel and Saul in his formative years. These encounters provided foundational revelation upon which David would ultimately build his tabernacle.

Let's take a glimpse back into David's origin story, beginning with the prophet Samuel. Samuel emerged as a prophet to Israel after a season where God was not speaking at all (1 Samuel 3:1, 19-21), and he would end up anointing Saul and David as Israel's first two kings.

Samuel was a forerunner who laid the foundations for the tabernacle of David by training up prophetic musicians, who would later serve as the staff for David's day-and-night worship tent. He did this by establishing "schools" of prophetic musicians among the Levites in the years preceding David's reign (1 Samuel 10:5-13, 19:18-24). Some believe that Samuel's team of prophetic musicians may have been the very first "band" of musicians in ancient history.[1]

---

1   I have heard this idea attributed to the research of Ray Hughes, but I also found this idea, without a citation, in Chris Burns, *Pioneers of His Presence* (Self-published, 2014), 74.

In the first of these stories, the prophetic musicians were described as coming down from a high place (1 Samuel 10:5). Most commentators agree that the worshipers were descending from a hill where they would have been offering priestly sacrifices and burnt offerings to God.[2] Samuel was a Levite who had learned to minister to God as a priest from his youth (1 Samuel 3:1), and he was teaching these minstrels to be priests and prophets with their music. Priesthood and prophecy flow together, and most Old Testament prophets were Levites. This makes sense, because a priest is someone who ministers to God and serves as a mediator between God and man. Levites like Samuel would spend time in God's presence through worship, prayer, and study of the Torah (God's word). Their relationship with God enabled them to prophesy—to hear God's voice and to speak to others on God's behalf.

Samuel acted as a spiritual father to these Levitical musicians, laying a foundation of discipleship and training that would be vital to keep the tabernacle of David sustained. He imparted this calling to minister to the Lord and prophesy to the next generation. He willingly spent his ministry raising up other young prophets, which allowed him to leave a legacy that lasted beyond his lifetime. This pattern would continue in the tabernacle of David, with some of Samuel's children serving as key musicians in David's tent (see 1 Chronicles 25:6). Both Saul and David's encounters with these prophetic minstrels would be life changing.

Saul's Failed Leadership

Saul was the very first king chosen by Israel. Before that time, Yahweh Himself had acted as the King of His people. God granted His people's request for a new king, and Samuel anointed Saul as

---

2   See comments on 1 Samuel 10:5 from *Joseph Benson's Commentary,* *Matthew Poole's Commentary* and *Gill's Exposition of the Bible.*

the first human king of Israel. After he was anointed, God's first instruction to King Saul was to visit the prophetic worship school (1 Samuel 10:5-6). What an interesting first assignment as the first king of Israel! Why would God tell Samuel to instruct Saul to go down to the prophetic musicians as his first lesson in how to be a king? Why would prophetic music be at the top of the agenda? It seems that Saul needed additional skill sets in preparation for his new leadership role.

When Saul encountered these prophetic minstrels, the Scriptures say "the spirit of God rushed upon Him" (1 Samuel 10:10). He was "turned into another man" (I Samuel 10:6), and God "gave him another heart" (1 Samuel 10:9). This priestly, prophetic music created an atmosphere of God's presence that dramatically changed the lives of those who encountered it. Samuel and his teams understood the reality that God is enthroned on praises, and God was letting the new king of Israel experience this power firsthand.

In his initial encounter with the prophetic musicians, I believe God was immediately trying to teach Saul how His kingdom works. There is something about musical, prophetic worship that is central to the way God's kingdom flows and functions. There is something about the priesthood and prophecy that is related to God's government. Saul would have to learn about worship if he wanted to be a leader in God's kingdom.

Unfortunately, he did not learn his lesson. Saul was not a successful king. Over the course of his reign, he constantly refused to walk in full obedience with a heart of worship towards God. He became proud and self-reliant. After one successful battle, Saul became impatient waiting for Samuel. He took the priesthood into His own hands and offered burnt offerings in contradiction to God's word. Samuel arrived with a rebuke from

God that Saul's kingly line would not continue. Instead, Samuel said, God would seek "a man after his own heart" (1 Samuel 13:14). That man was David.

Another string of mistakes would culminate with Saul's final act of disobedience. Rather than annihilating the Amalekites as God instructed, he kept some of their animals for himself. When Samuel arrived to confront Saul in his disobedience, Saul lied and said that they were going to be sacrificed as burnt offerings to God. Samuel rebuked him and told him that "to obey is better than to sacrifice" (1 Samuel 15:22). Saul tried to cover up his inward selfishness with external religious activity (sacrifice), but God wanted nothing to do with it. God wanted Saul's heart (obedience). Yet Saul was a self-seeking king who wanted to rule in his own way rather than serve as a conduit through which God could lead Israel. At that point, God rejected Saul and promised the end of his reign.

David is Anointed as King

Immediately following this episode, Samuel was led by God to anoint a new king of Israel. David was the man after God's heart who had been chosen to replace Saul. As soon as David was anointed king, Scripture says "the Spirit of the Lord rushed upon David from that day forward." (1 Samuel 16:14). How would this lingering presence of the Holy Spirit empower David? In the very next verse God sent a distressing spirit to torment King Saul. David was invited to come play his harp to soothe Saul and bring relief to his oppression.

And so it was, whenever the spirit from God was upon Saul, that David would take a harp and play it with his hand. Then Saul would become refreshed and well, and the distressing spirit would depart from him (1 Samuel 16:23).

When David played his harp, God's presence and power would manifest to relieve Saul from the demonic torment. What Saul had experienced with Samuel's prophetic worship schools, he was experiencing again through David's music—the reality that praise brings God's presence, and God's presence changes everything.

It is remarkable that after both Saul and David were anointed as kings, the very first thing that happened was a demonstration of the power of prophetic worship! Saul was anointed and immediately encountered Samuel's worship schools and was "turned into another man." David was anointed king and immediately played his harp and saw the demons flee from the king. Again, it raises the question: why would the Spirit of God want to teach the kings of Israel about the power of musical worship as their first leadership lessons?

What David learned, but Saul never did, is that the atmosphere of God's kingdom is actually prophetic, musical worship and prayer; that kingdom authority flows from worship. Saul was still technically king, but David suddenly had more authority. Even with all the power and resources of his position, Saul could not deliver himself from the demonic torment of the spirits that harassed him. But one shepherd boy who was surrendered to God, who had learned to move God's heart with his songs, could play his harp and set the king free. Saul had earthly position, but David had heavenly authority.

Essentially, God was trying to help Saul and David both realize that they could never rightfully rule and reign over Israel. Yahweh Himself was the one who could truly walk in the authority needed to lead the nation. However, if they would learn that God is "enthroned in praise" (Psalm 22:3), then they could allow God to have his rightful place in the kingdom. Because of Saul's pride and selfishness, he never wanted to submit to the leadership of the Lord. His heart was hardened by arrogance and rebellion, so he refused to worship God. Instead, Saul was committed to enthroning himself as king. Yet David's heart was tender towards God. He surrendered his heart and leadership to the leadership of the Lord. He recognized that prophetic worship opened the door to God's presence, bringing the kingdom of God with it. David was learning that, in God's kingdom, proper priestly activity was vital to ensuring proper kingly activity. I believe God tried to teach Saul this from the very start, but he never received it.

We see this same principle in heaven. The twenty-four elders that circle the throne room "cast down their crowns" before God Himself (Revelation 4:10). They give up their authority and enthrone the only One who is worthy of it all. You will either willingly cast down your crown like David or be forced to cast down your crown like Saul. For those with a humble heart like David, like those twenty-four elders, they receive access to the very throne of God. They have true authority because they have humility. In the next scene in heaven, those same elders are not wearing crowns anymore, but are holding harps and bowls of incense, which represent the prayers of God's people (Revelation 5:8). The kings have become priests. This was also the path that David took.

Saul wanted to be a king, but David desired to be a priest. Saul ended up being neither and David ended up doing both. There is a way authority works in God's kingdom, and Saul missed it. David got it. God's government flows from worship. Authority comes from intimacy. David had the heart of a worshiper. He wanted what God wanted. And if we want to see God's kingdom come on earth as in heaven (Matthew 6:10), we must avoid doing things Saul's way and miss it all.

worshipped —▷ Enthroned —▷
release His authority/power. Sing a New Song.

A Final Encounter with the School of Prophets

As the years progressed, God's favor was clearly resting upon David instead of Saul. David led the nation into numerous victories on the battlefield, and the people of Israel began to respond to his anointed leadership and true authority. As his influence waned, Saul became jealous. His anger and resentment grew into hatred, until Saul desired to kill David.

When Saul became distressed by a demonic spirit again (that will happen when you allow jealousy and hatred to grow in your heart), David again tried to play his harp for Saul. Refusing to receive deliverance, Saul threw his spear at David (1 Samuel 19:9-10). David narrowly escaped and fled to Ramah to visit Samuel.

Saul sent messengers after David, but they kept running into Samuel's prophetic worship bands. Each time, the presence of God would overtake them and they would begin to prophesy along with the minstrels! Saul had still not learned the power of God's presence. After three teams of messengers all were overtaken in the atmosphere created by these musical Levites, Saul himself went to visit David.

> *So he went there to Naioth in Ramah. Then the Spirit of God was upon him also, and he went on and prophesied until he came to Naioth in Ramah. And he also stripped off his clothes and prophesied before Samuel in like manner, and lay down naked all that day and all that night. Therefore they say, "Is Saul also among the prophets?"*
> *(1 Samuel 19:23-24).*

Saul was humiliated. All his effort and earthly authority could not overtake a tribe of wholehearted worshipers armed with nothing more than their instruments. Saul still had not learned the ways of the kingdom of God or the power of God's presence!

Chris Burns says, *"Prophetic worship turns killers into prophets and kings into fools!"*[3] The King appears when we worship, and anything lifted up against God's authority will cast down in His presence. Again, God was demonstrating to Saul and David the ways of His kingdom.

The visit at Ramah was the only time David is recorded as interacting with Samuel, other than his initial anointing as king. However, David was profoundly influenced by these prophetic musicians and his own experience of playing the harp before Saul. God was laying the groundwork for David's tabernacle. Some have proposed that David could have received the vision and blueprint for his tabernacle during his visit to Samuel at Ramah.[4] While we can't confirm that hypothesis, I am sure that David's experience with Samuel's band of prophetic musicians had a lasting impact on David's life and leadership. God was preparing him to become a unique ruler of Israel who would lead the nation into a taste of heaven on earth.

Prophetic Worship and A New Song

It's worth noting that Samuel's prophetic musicians were not just offering praises to God. The story says specifically that they were prophesying. There is something about *prophetic* worship in particular that creates an environment of God's manifest presence and power. There is nothing wrong with singing prewritten songs, but I believe God also wants the church to sing songs that are spontaneous and prophetic.

Throughout the Psalms you find God inviting His people to sing to Him a "new song" (Psalm 33:3, 40:3, 96:1, 98:1, 144:9, 149:1). I believe the Old Testament "new song" is similar to what

---

3   Burns, *Pioneers of His Presence,* 76.
4   Billy Humphrey, *Unceasing,* 2nd ed. (Kansas City, MO: Forerunner Publishing, 2009, 2015), 25-27.

the New Testament calls a "spiritual song" (Ephesians 5:18-20, Colossians 3:16). There is something about a spontaneous song that invites us to connect our hearts and minds more deeply to what we are singing. It forces a worshiper beyond the regurgitation of words and melody and into singing to Him from our own hearts.

While singing "psalms and hymns" in church is not uncommon, in my experience, the phenomenon of singing "spiritual songs" to God is rare in many Christian traditions. Yet it is emphasized clearly in Scripture, and it seems to be connected uniquely to the manifestation of God's presence and power amid praise and worship.

One of my favorite Hebrew words for praise is *tehillah*, which means singing from your heart to the Lord. Many times when the Bible refers to a "new song," it is accompanied by *tehillah* (see Ps. 40:3, Isaiah 42:10). In the

Isaiah prophesies of a global "tehillah" worship movement that will flood the earth with new songs prior to the return of Jesus.

Bible, tehillah is connected to the major passages in Psalms about experiencing God's manifest presence. We "Enter His courts with praise [tehillah]" (Psalm 100:4). God is "enthroned in the praises [tehillah]" of His people (Psalm 22:3). Because of how God's presence manifested so powerfully when they sang, I believe Samuel's prophetic worship leaders were probably offering *tehillah* to God as well.

Isaiah prophesies of a global "tehillah" worship movement that will flood the earth with new songs prior to the return of Jesus. As the nations have a revelation of Christ, they will respond with songs of thanksgiving. In every geographic place, spiritual songs of praise and adoration will be ringing out to the Lord. I note where "tehilah" is featured in the passage from Isaiah 42 below.

"I am the Lord; that is my name; my glory I give to no other, nor my praise [tehillah] to carved idols...."
Sing to the Lord a new song, his praise [tehillah] from the end of the earth, you who go down to the sea, and all that fills it, the coastlands and their inhabitants. Let the desert and its cities lift up their voice, the villages... let them shout from the top of the mountains.
Let them give glory to the Lord, and declare his praise [tehillah] in the coastlands (Isaiah 42:8-12).

Can you imagine the entire body of Christ operating in the same transformative power as Samuel's team of prophetic musicians? What if the whole world was filled with "new songs" that ushered in God's manifest presence? I believe it's coming. In response to the worth of Jesus, "tehillah" will flood the earth!

In Scripture, the word "tehillah" is also connected to God's salvation of the nations. The first instance of tehillah is the spontaneous song after God takes the Israelites through the Red Sea and delivers them from the Egyptians (Exodus 15:11). The very first song that was sung when David set up his tabernacle speaks about the nations offering "tehillah" to the Lord.

"Save us, O God of our salvation, and gather and deliver us from among the nations, that we may give thanks to your holy name and glory in your praise [tehillah]"
(1 Chronicles 16:35).

Already, we are seeing hints that God's purposes for praise and worship are far greater than for having good church services. There is something bigger going on. As we will continue to explore in later chapters, there are deep connections between the release of prophetic worship in the nations, the manifestation of God's presence, and God's purposes in fulfilling the Great Commission.

The Procession

*And I will be even more undignified than this, and will be
humble in my own sight (2 Samuel 6:22).*

As we have already seen clearly, David's burning passion was to be
close to God. This was the desire of his heart. In the secret place,
David had experienced intimacy with the Lord. He discovered the
power of God's presence through praise and worship. Between
playing his harp before Saul and Samuel's school of minstrels, he
had seen how the atmosphere could be shifted through prophetic
songs. So when God appointed David as King, the culture of the
kingdom would reflect these values, priorities, and passions. What
David experienced personally began to manifest corporately.

The Procession of the Ark

David had decided that Jerusalem would be the new capital
of Israel, and he also located the ark of the covenant, which
was previously stationed at the town of Kiriath-Jearim. David
understood that the Ark was the place where the nation of Israel
was privileged to get a taste of heaven on the earth.[1] God's
presence and voice flowed from between the cherubim on top of
this golden box (Samuel 6:2, 1 Chronicles 13:6). If David wanted

---

1   G.K. Beale, *The Temple and the Church's Mission* (Madison, WI: Intervarsity Press Adademic, 2004), 112.

his nation to publicly experience God's presence the way he had in private, he needed to put the ark in the center of the life of their kingdom and establish constant praise and worship in their city. This was David's top priority as the new king of a united Israel.

After some brief deliberation with his military leaders, David was ready to proceed. They would gather all Israel in a great procession to bring the ark of the covenant into Jerusalem (1 Chronicles 13:1-4). It was time for Israel to host the presence of God. Just as the Philistines had returned the Ark to Israel on a cart (I Samuel 6), David set the ark on a new cart to journey up the mountain of Zion, where David had established his palace. The worship procession had begun!

David again gathered all the chosen men of Israel, thirty thousand. And David arose and went with all the people who were with him from Baale-judah to bring up from there the ark of God, which is called by the name of the Lord of hosts who sits enthroned on the cherubim. And they carried the ark of God on a new cart.... (2 Samuel 6:1-4).

But David's first attempt to transport the ark failed. As the ark was being carried on a cart, pulled by oxen, the oxen stumbled. Uzzah touched the ark to steady it and died instantly. (2 Samuel 6:6, 1 Chronicles 13:9). In fear, David took the ark and left it at Obed Edom's house (who was a Gentile, curiously). Obed-Edom's house was blessed by the presence of the ark of the covenant as it rested there for three months before David would try again.

The ark of the Lord remained in the house of Obed-Edom the Gittite for three months. And the Lord blessed Obed-Edom and all his household (2 Samuel 6:11).

I often wonder what happened in David's heart and life during those three months while the ark rested at Obed-Edom's home.

Interestingly, the 1 Chronicles account breaks up David's story after the ark rests at Obed-Edom's house, and it takes chapter 14 to tell the story of David fighting two battles. Before each of these battles it says that David "inquired of God" (1 Chron. 14:10,14) for a battle strategy. Each time God gave David a different plan, and each time he was victorious.

The timeline is not clear about whether the battles took place before or after David's first attempt to bring the ark to Jerusalem.[2] But either way, I believe the Chronicler is trying to teach us something about the three-month delay. David had to learn to follow God's voice and His ways. He had to remember to "inquire of God" for every step along his journey. Just as David's victories in battle were dependent on "inquiring of God," he would also need to seek God for every step of the establishment of his tabernacle of worship in Jerusalem. God had a unique plan for David. Hearing and obeying the voice of the Lord would be vital.

After reviewing God's laws, David remembered that the ark was to be carried on the shoulders of Levites, not on an ox cart. The ox represents the strength of humanity and the cart represents man's way of doing things. God was helping David understand that His presence was only to be hosted by true worshipers. No man-made structure or system would suffice to house the manifest presence of God. It was the hearts, lives, and praise of consecrated worshipers (in this case, the Levites) who could "carry" the glory of God into their city.

When David saw Obed-Edom being blessed by the presence of the ark for three months, he finally decided to try again to carry it to Jerusalem (2 Samuel 6:12). But for round two, a few

---

2   2 Samuel is organized differently than 1 Chronicles. It places the battles in chapter 5, before bringing the ark into the city. The narrative in 2 Samuel 6 goes immediately into David's second attempt to bring the ark into Jerusalem.

things had changed. First, David pitched a tent and prepared a place for the ark. Second, David commanded that the ark should be carried on the shoulders of the Levites, not an ox cart.

> David built houses for himself in the city of David. And he prepared a place for the ark of God and pitched a tent for it. Then David said that no one but the Levites may carry the ark of God, for the Lord had chosen them to carry the ark of the Lord and to minister to him forever. And David assembled all Israel at Jerusalem to bring up the ark of the Lord to its place, which he had prepared for it (1 Chronicles 15:1-3).

For the second worship parade, David brought up the ark again—this time carried by Levites—offering burnt sacrifices to God every six steps. This procession was a massive celebration with extravagant offerings of worship. It says David assembled "all the house Israel" (2 Samuel 6:15) as he "went and brought up the ark of God from the house of Obed-Edom to the City of David with gladness." (6:12) David "danced before the Lord with all his might" (6:14) and was seen "leaping and whirling before the Lord" (6:16). The Levitical musicians were appointed "to be the singers accompanied by instruments of music, stringed instruments, harps, and cymbals, by raising the voice with resounding joy" (1 Chronicles 15:16). This was an elaborate parade of burnt offerings, music, and celebration. Can you imagine the sounds, sights, and smells as they marched ten miles from Obed-Edom's house to their capital city?

They eventually reached the pinnacle of Mt Zion and set the ark into the new tent beside King David's palace. They offered a final burnt offering (this would be the very last burnt offering ever offered at David's tabernacle), and then they distributed a meal to all the people. The burnt offerings had ceased, the procession had ended, and the people returned to their homes. Yet the songs of praise around the ark continued. David had appointed musicians to remain before the ark to worship the Lord day and night.

Why This Waste?

The joy of this special day came to an abrupt halt when David returned home. David's wife Michal did not appreciate David's enthusiasm for God's presence, or the way he involved himself in the priesthood of Israel.

> *Now as the ark of the Lord came into the City of David, Michal, Saul's daughter, looked through a window and saw King David leaping and whirling before the Lord; and she despised him in her heart....And Michal the daughter of Saul came out to meet David, and said, "How glorious was the king of Israel today, uncovering himself today in the eyes of the maids of his servants, as one of the base fellows shamelessly uncovers himself!" (v.16, 20).*

David had set aside his "kingliness" in order to worship with the common people and to serve as a priest for all of the nation. Rather than wearing his crown, he wore an ephod, a priestly garment (2 Samuel 6:14), to make way for the King of Kings. He wanted to give people access to God's presence, so he humbled himself dramatically during the procession of the ark. He rejoiced with abandon that God's glory would be in the center of his kingdom. David ultimately recognized that God was to be the true king of Israel.

His wife was offended that someone of high regard such as the king would humble himself as David did. Something inside her resented the extravagant worship that David offered God as he danced and sang in the streets. After this altercation, Michal was never able to bear children again (v.23).

Likewise, I believe the fruit of the religious spirit is barrenness in one's soul. Fear, accusation, and judgement caused by prideful religion causes the flow of spiritual life in our hearts to become barren. Our hearts become hard when we judge the worship of others instead of humbling ourselves, focusing on the Lord and joining in the celebration.

For radical worshipers, many times the passion and pursuit of God's presence is misunderstood or shunned by those around us, and sometimes by those very close to us; especially anyone under the influence of a religious spirit. This is not shocking. Hell hates the presence of God. Religiosity reacts strongly to extravagant expressions of worship and attempts to create fear that hinders freedom and joy. The enemy accuses the radical worshiper by asking "Why this waste?" Why should David offer a burnt offering every six steps along the way to Jerusalem? Why did he have to gather all of Israel and go to such great expense to usher God's presence into his city? Why such a big deal over the ark? Didn't David need to deal with the economy and the military? Didn't he need to maintain his place of dignity and notoriety as the king of Israel?

This is not the only time in the Scriptures where extravagant worship stirred up controversy. The woman who broke the alabaster jar of perfume upon Jesus is one of the clearest examples of this same principle.

> *Now when Jesus was at Bethany in the house of Simon the leper, a woman came up to him with an alabaster flask of very expensive ointment, and she poured it on his head as he re-clined at table. And when the disciples saw it, they were indig-nant, saying, "Why this waste? (Matthew 26:6-8).*

"Why this waste?" In response to a lavish demonstration of

devotion, the enemy mocked with accusations of foolish excess. But Jesus affirmed the sacrificial offering of love and called it a "beautiful thing" (Matthew 26:9). Throughout the Bible, God always defends extravagant expressions of worship and those who prioritize His presence. Whether it is King David's undignified worship, Mary who sat at the feet of Jesus, or the woman who poured the alabaster jar of perfume on Jesus's feet, costly expressions of worship were always celebrated by the Lord.

The Cost of Extravagant Worship

When our group of friends set out on our journey to become "undignified," we experienced a small measure of hardship in pursuing extravagant worship. When I initially came back from my camp encounter and began to share the vision of our 6:22 worship nights. I proposed that we do two hours of worship every Friday night. I was told by mentors that it was excessive. I was encouraged to consider doing monthly worship nights or maybe doing just one hour each week. I was told it was unlikely that teenagers would gather for two hours of musical worship every week. This was 2002, and dedicated worship nights were far less common than they are now.

It was hard to receive pushback, particularly from influential spiritual leaders in my life. Yet I stuck to the vision God had given me, driven by a passion for more of God, and for my generation to experience God's presence. After we launched, God began to move powerfully. Within a few months, we found ourselves lingering for three or more hours many Friday nights. The two hours that initially seemed "excessive" were now not enough. Students would be laid out on the floor "soaking" in God's presence or weeping from encountering His love. Many didn't want to leave.

Our meetings were not without controversy. After a few

months, I received a call from a local youth pastor who scolded me for trying to "steal" students from his Friday night youth gathering. I tried to explain that we were uniting students from many different churches, but he still saw us as competition. As a nineteen-year-old young leader, this kind of criticism affected me deeply. When God began to manifest his power, some people labeled us as a cult. We were pioneering new expressions of worship, prayer, and creativity, and those who were stuck in their ways did not appreciate it. Certain pastors even encouraged people from their pulpits not to associate with us. As I entertained these accusations in my heart, I began to question what God had called me to do. It felt like they were throwing water on the fire of my heart, and I wondered if I had made a huge mistake.

I must also point out that there were many pastors and leaders who were supportive of us during that time as well; but of course, it was easy to focus on the few who were against us and get discouraged. We did our best to hold tight to God's affirmation that our radical worship and prayer was a "beautiful thing" to Jesus. The way God manifested His presence and power at our meetings also provided a blessing from heaven that gave us strength to move forward despite the challenges. Like David, we were determined to prioritize God's presence and worship Him with all our hearts.

The Priority of God's Presence

This undignified procession of the ark was one of David's first acts as king of a united Israel. David's agenda was focused on getting to Mt Zion to establish his kingdom and to bring God's manifest presence right into the center of their nation. With an unbelievable amount of leadership pressure on his shoulders, David went out of His way to lead the nation into a new season of worship.

The military was important. The economy was important. But for David, the presence was most important. He would shift Israel's resources, time, and money to make sure the ark was nearby, and to provide the Levites with funds and training to properly host the presence of God with day and night worship.

Can you imagine a modern-day equivalent of this? What would be the reaction if a president or prime minister hired worship leaders to sing day and night in the legislative halls of the nations of the earth? What if leaders of governments began to say that they did not want to govern until Jesus was receiving praise in their nation day and night? My friends in Washington DC have a ministry called David's Tent DC, where they have a literal tent of non-stop musical worship and prayer that has been going since September 2015. How radical would it be if the federal government budgeted the funds to employ the workers to staff that tent? I understand that Israel was called to be a theocracy, so the comparisons break down a bit. But David's prioritization of God's presence took radical intentionality. Even for ancient Israel, David's leadership approach was revolutionary.

I believe God is inviting the body of Christ to reorient around His presence. Whether in homes, churches, cities, tents, or nations, the very person and presence of God must take center stage again. We are beginning to see the emergence of presence-centered communities around the world, but currently they are a minority. Most Christian activity in the western church is still man-centered. Ministries are either built around felt needs and programs to make people feel comfortable, or around charismatic personalities and celebrity "ministers." Certainly, we want to serve and love others, but we must not neglect God Himself in the process. If we have people in the seats but God is not present, no one's life will ever be changed. It's not our efforts, programs, songs, words, and presence that bring transformation. It is beholding the beauty of Jesus that takes us from glory to glory (2 Corinthians 3:18).

In the days ahead, God is going to raise up bold leaders like David who are unafraid to prioritize the presence of God. Ministry to the Lord will fuel ministry to others. Extravagant expressions of worship and prayer will be normalized in local communities. Jesus said His house would be called a "house of prayer." In the future, the reputation of the church will be that we are a people marked by ongoing interaction with God. As the Lord imparts the spirit of David's tabernacle, hours and hours of worship and prayer will be happening throughout the week in many cities across the earth. And rather than becoming a hindrance to reaching people, God's joyful presence will become the very magnet that draws the seeking hearts to Jesus. Have we forgotten that in God's presence there is fullness of joy (Ps. 16:11)? Who would not be attracted to the most joyful and pleasure-filled place in the world: the place of God's presence?

Even More Undignified Than This

The entire procession of the Ark of the covenant points us to a greater reality. Just as David humbled himself to worship with the common people of Israel, Jesus humbled himself to come to earth to dwell with humanity. He humbled himself even to the point of death on a cross for our sins (Philippians 2:5-8). As David marched the ark up to Mt Zion, offering animal sacrifices every six steps, there was probably a trail of blood that flowed from Zion down into the rest of the city. And as Christ carried his cross up the mount of Golgotha, there was likewise a trail of blood flowing down the mountain and into Israel—blood that was shed for the sins of mankind.

Perhaps David had a hint of what was to come. When Michael

brought the accusation against him, his response was puzzling:

"I will become even more undignified than this"
(2 Samuel 6:22).

When exactly did David become "more undignified," by the way? There is no other story of David dancing wildly; no other account of a great procession in the narrative of King David.

I believe that David was prophesying of the Son of David, the King of Kings, who would bring the ark (God's presence) into the midst of His people, suffering reproach, bearing the shame of a cross and becoming "even more undignified" than David. He was totally abandoned to His Father's will. He totally surrendered and only did what He saw his Father doing (John 5:1-23). And just as David made a way for Israel to access God's presence, Jesus has made a way for all the nations to enter God's presence.

5

Davidic Worship

The story of King David carrying the ark of the covenant into Jerusalem with "undignified" worship was foundational for our local worship community. For years I had never taken the time to look at the biblical context, so I had never noticed that David was transporting the ark into a brand-new 24/7 worship tent.[1] The ark's great procession was not just as a one-time event, but rather a means to an end—to host God's manifest presence in an ongoing way in the center of their nation. The climax of this story was the ark being placed in a tent on Mount Zion. David's longing was always for a dwelling place in Israel for God Himself to be present with His people, and the undignified worship was actually a forerunner to day-and-night worship. As I began to study this progression in Scripture, I felt myself drawn into a greater narrative that seemed significant to our ministry and to the church at large.

A Third Tabernacle

Despite the pervasive impact of David's worship and kingdom

---

1   Part of the reason I had never noticed this narrative was because I was using 2 Samuel 6 as our reference point for David's journey. The books of Samuel have very few details about David's tabernacle. However, the book of 1 Chronicles tells the same story, except it includes the details of the tabernacle of David. When I discovered this parallel story, I realized that there was so much more happening than I initially realized.

on the biblical narrative, many believers go their whole lives without ever hearing one sermon on David's tabernacle. Even many Bible commentators fail to note the significance of the story. David's tabernacle is the primary subject of the entire book of 1 Chronicles and the birthplace of many of the Psalms. Every great revival throughout Israel's history refers back to the worship order David established at his tent. Two of Israel's prophets speak of its restoration (Amos 9:11 and Isaiah 16:5). There is no prophetic promise that Moses's tabernacle or Solomon's temple will be rebuilt; but David's will. David's tabernacle is so significant that it keeps resurfacing throughout the Scriptures, such as at the first major church council (Acts 15:16-17).

Understanding David's tabernacle has profound implications on how we relate to God, how we function as the church, and how we accomplish God's mission in the world. But before getting too deep into its implications, let's look more closely at the tent David established. Before we can understand the restoration of David's tabernacle and its effect on our lives, we need to understand the original David's tabernacle. I want you to see it clearly. What exactly was happening under that tent on a hillside in Jerusalem three thousand years ago?

Access to God's Presence

One of the unique features of David's tabernacle is its simplicity of structure. There is an odd lack of rooms, decor and furniture. Reading through the description of Moses's tabernacle in Exodus, one sees the intricate stipulations regarding the sizes, materials, and colors of every element. The most talented artists were recruited to create an elaborate sanctuary in which the priests and Levites would serve the Lord. Yet, unlike Moses's tabernacle, there is minimal description of the physical structure of David's tent. The story simply mentions "the tent that David had pitched for it" (1 Chronicles 15:1, 16:1).

In Moses's tabernacle, the ark was hidden in an inner chamber called the Holy of Holies. The only person who would come into direct contact with the ark would be the high priest who would offer sacrifices on the annual Day of Atonement (see Leviticus 16).

And the Lord said to Moses, "Tell Aaron your brother not to come at any time into the Holy Place inside the veil, before the mercy seat that is on the ark, so that he may not die. For I will appear in the cloud over the mercy seat" (Leviticus 16:2).

Needless to say, there was a measure of the fear of the Lord surrounding this mysterious and powerful piece of furniture. The kingdom of Israel was acutely aware of the power and danger that came with mishandling the manifest presence of God. The death of Uzzah during their first attempt at bringing the Ark into Jerusalem (1 Chronicles 13:9-10) served as a potent reminder. With this so fresh in their memory, you would think that the nation would be wary of direct access to this ark. Yet, in David's tabernacle, there is no mention of a veil in front of the ark at all. It seems that the ark of the covenant was

> In the tent of David, God's people are invited to stand right in front of the ark of the covenant—to experience His presence at any time.

accessible. The Levites are described as ministering "before the ark of the Lord" (1 Chronicles 16:2, 37). The contrast with Leviticus 16:2 is stunning. In the tent of David, God's people are invited to stand right in front of the ark of the covenant—to experience His presence at any time. In contrast with the Mosaic tabernacle, David's tabernacle shifts the emphasis from the physical structure to the presence of God and the worshipers themselves.

The Centrality of the Musicians

Those worshipers were the Levites. The revolutionary praise and worship of David's tabernacle was sustained for thirty-three years by a community of Levitical musicians and singers who provided the "service of song" before the ark of the covenant (1 Chronicles 6:31-32). Their job was "to minister before the ark of the Lord, to commemorate, to thank, and to praise the Lord God" (1 Chronicles 16:4). The Levitical musicians and their prophetic songs were at the core of the purpose of David's tabernacle. Previously the musicians had been relegated to the prophetic fringe of Israel—such as the teams that Samuel trained on the hills (I Samuel 10:5-13, 19:18-24). Yet when David came into power, the songs of the hillsides took center stage in the worship activity of the nation. The centrality of the Levitical musicians and singers in 1 Chronicles highlights the importance of musical worship to David's reign. Even the geneologies put the musicians right in the center.

> *"The center of the center of the genealogy is a list of Levitical musicians and singers appointed by David….To be a priestly nation is, by the Chronicler's lights, to be a choral nation. Israel fulfills its role among the nations through a continuous liturgy of praise…. Musicians are at the center. At the edges of the geneology are kings…. the king guards the boundaries of Israel to protect Israel's central activity, which is worship."[2]*

As soon David arrived on Mount Zion with the ark, the musicians began their songs (1 Chronicles 16). It is not clear exactly how many musicians and singers were already trained at the launch of David's tabernacle, but by the time David passed off the kingdom to his son Solomon, Israel had a remarkable 4,000

---

2   Peter J. Leithart, *1 & 2 Chronicles* (Grand Rapids, MI: Brazos Press, 2019), 12.

musicians at their disposal (1 Chronicles 23:5). It appears from the story that at least some of the musicians of David's tabernacle lived together in a community near the tent, ministering to God together and trusting Him for their provision.

> Now these, the singers, the heads of fathers' houses of the **Levites, were in the chambers of the temple free from other service, for they were on duty day and night.** These were heads of fathers' houses of the Levites, according to their generations, leaders. These lived in Jerusalem (1 Chronicles 9:33-34).

At least some of the musicians, specifically the "heads of the fathers' houses," were living in Jerusalem and "free from other duties" while serving at the tent full-time. David allocated massive amounts of financial resources to staffing and maintaining the day and night worship—both from his personal treasury and from the nation's wealth (1 Chronicles 29:1-9).

The Twenty-four Divisions of Singers

1 Chronicles 25 describes those who provided leadership for the worship in the tent. They "prophesied with lyres, with harps, and with cymbals" (1 Chronicles 25:1) and were "under the direction of their father for the music in the house of the Lord, with cymbals, stringed instruments, and harps… The number of them along with their brothers, who were trained in singing to the Lord, all who were skillful, was 288" (1 Chronicles 25:6-7). It says that Asaph, Jeduthun and Heman, along with David, served as the primary musical and spiritual "fathers" of David's tabernacle. Their twenty-four sons were the primary team leaders who each led a team of twelve prophetic singers and musicians—giving us the 288 total prophetic singers. Each team was "under the direction" of their fathers for relational, musical, and spiritual

discipleship. It's important to note this process of mentoring and multiplication. I believe this culture of spiritual and musical fathering was David's strategy to keep the tent of day-and-night worship in place for the entire thirty-three years of his reign. There must have been ongoing training and equipping of the musicians throughout those decades.

Some who teach on David's tabernacle assume that the twenty-four teams must have been in place to cover the twenty-four hours of the day.[3] While this may initially seems like a great idea, the understanding of a twenty-four hour day was non-existent in the days of King David. It was Hipparchus who proposed dividing the day into twenty-four equal parts in the second century BC— around 800 years after King David! The twenty-four divisions of musicians at David's tent described in 1 Chronicles 25 mirror the divisions of the Levitical priests described in the previous chapter (1 Chronicles 24). These divisions corresponded to twenty-four weeks, not the hours in a day. Each division would then come to Jerusalem and serve for one week, every twenty-four weeks. Biblical and historical evidence seems to show that each division would serve for eight days, with an overlap of two divisions on each Sabbath.

> *The Levites and all Judah did according to all that Jehoiada the priest commanded, and they each brought his men, who were to go off duty on the Sabbath, with those who were to come on duty on the Sabbath, for Jehoiada the priest did not dismiss the divisions (2 Chronicles 23:8).*

The historian Josephus acknowledged this same system,

---

3   See David Fritch *Enthroned: Bringing God's Kingdom to Earth Through Unceasing Worship & Prayer* (Independently published, 2017), 46 and John Dickson and Chuck D. Pierce, *Worship As It Is In Heaven* (Ventura, CA: Gospel Light, 2010), 101-102.

where they would come into Jerusalem for eight days to serve their week at the tabernacle:

"David... divided them also into courses: and when he had separated the priests from them, he found of these priests twenty-four courses... and that course which came up first was written down as the first, and accordingly the second, and so on to the twenty-fourth; and this partition hath remained to this day. He also made twenty-four parts of the tribe of Levi; and when they cast lots, they came up in the same manner for their courses of <u>eight days</u>." [4]

This week-long service is also what is described with the twenty-four divisions of gatekeepers (1 Chronicles 9:22-27). The gatekeepers had to keep their "office of trust" or sacred trust. This was their appointed time to serve at the house of the Lord. Groups of gatekeepers would come in for their week of the "sacred trust" to live in Jerusalem and collectively guard the tabernacle day and night. Then they would return to their "villages" when the next group arrived for the following week of service.

> A culture of spiritual and musical fathering was David's strategy to keep the tent of day-and-night worship in place for the entire thirty-three years of his reign.

It is unlikely that there were 4,000 full-time musicians constantly living in Jerusalem. Rather, the divisions of Levitical musicians would rotate into Jerusalem on a weekly basis to serve at David's tent. Like a bi-annual "missions trip," most of the Levitical families would take a pilgrimage to the capital city to

---

4   Josephus, *Antiquities of the Jews,* Book 7, chapter 14:7.

serve the Lord with their songs each year. Perhaps some of the fathers and key musicians lived on-site constantly, as 1 Chronicles 9:33 indicates, to provide ongoing oversight and administration of the operation. Collectively these musical teams would sustain the constant offerings of praise to the Lord.

Musical Sacrifices of Praise

The musical expression of Levitical ministry was a profound shift in the understanding and culture of worship for God's people. The sacrifices of Moses's tabernacle were burnt offerings as prescribed in the Torah. Yet there were no ongoing burnt offerings happening at David's tent on Mt Zion. David broke tradition by instructing the Levites to offer songs of praise as their offerings unto the Lord. Whereas Levites previously offered animal sacrifices, they now offered unceasing praise (Psalm 50:14, 23, 116:17, 141:2). David believed that praise and prayer, connected to a pure heart of worship, were the kind of sacrifices God desired. God spoke through Asaph, one of David's chief musicians, that "one who offers thanksgiving as his sacrifice glorifies me" (Psalm 50:23). In David's famous psalm of repentance, he acknowledged that God is not "pleased with a burnt offering" but is looking for the sacrifices of a "broken and contrite heart" (Psalm 51:16-17). He compared these expressions of praise and prayer to the priestly activities that were familiar to Israel. Centuries before the apostle John would see our prayers as "bowls of incense" in heaven (Revelation 5:8), David wrote that his prayers were "counted as incense" to the Lord and the lifting his hands in praise was like "the evening sacrifice" (Psalm 141:2). To David, praise was priestly, and the New Testament reinforces the fact that we, too, are to offer up a "sacrifice of praise" (Hebrews 13:15) to the Lord just as the Levites did.

Some say David introduced music as a form of sacrifice

because he himself was a musician, and he wanted to express his unique worship to the Lord. However, this revolution in Israel's worship was not because of David's personal preferences, but because he realized this is how God longs to be worshiped. Remember, David was a man after God's own heart (I Samuel 13:14). He wanted to please the Lord. Scripture declares that God himself sings (Zephaniah 3:17), and there are over 200 references to singing in the Bible. In the heavenly throne room, God is surrounded by elders who have harps (Revelation 5:8). Heaven is musical. God is musical. So it is natural that David's tabernacle was musical as well.

Excellence and Creativity

The Levitical musicians and singers that were appointed to praise God at David's tabernacle were not amateur artists. They were trained and skillful in their craft. A Levite named Chenaniah was put in charge of the singing for the ark's procession "because he was skillful" (1 Chronicles 15:22, NASB). The 288 singers who were specifically trained to sing and prophesy with their instruments were also described as "skillful" (1 Chronicles 25:7). Psalm 33:3 commanded the musicians to "play skillfully on the strings." Musical excellence was obviously a core value. If these musicians were going to be playing before God himself, they wanted to offer Him their best efforts.

> Heaven is musical. God is musical. So it is natural that David's tabernacle was musical as well.

The quality and quantity of the music was top priority for David and His kingdom. This musical enterprise was not a side gig for aspiring musicians or a haphazard jam session for Yahweh. This was a well-organized, high-quality musical project of an unprecedented scale, comparable to some of the greatest orchestras and music schools of human history. By the end of his reign as king, David and his team had trained 4,000 musicians (1 Chronicles 23:5) to supply an abundance of musical manpower for Solomon's temple that would soon succeed David's tabernacle.

In contrast to the simplicity and homeliness of the physical tent itself, the musicians, their instruments, and their songs were given much detail and attention. Creative energy and financial resources were spent in developing new sounds and fresh songs. There were string, wind, and percussion instruments, including some that David built and invented himself (1 Chronicles 23:5, Amos 6:5). If your vision of worship at David's tabernacle is an American worship leader with an acoustic guitar singing, "How Great Is Our God," then you need to let God's Word reinvigorate your imagination. These Jewish Levites were passionately celebrating God with a variety of musical instruments and styles (1 Chronicles 15:16, 28, Psalm 150). There was creativity, innovation, celebration, and dancing. All the biblical expressions of praise found throughout the Psalms[5] were on full display. It was loud (1 Chronicles 15:16, Psalm 150:5), noisy, creative, and beautiful!

All the biblical expressions of praise found throughout the Psalms were on full display. It was loud, noisy, creative, and beautiful!

Prophetic and Intercessory Worship

The music at David's tabernacle provided a unique prophetic atmosphere that was pioneered by Samuel and instituted by David, where God's heart could be expressed and declared. The worship leaders were not just trained to praise, but to prophesy

---

5   See chapter 2.

(1 Chronicles 25:1-3). David's tabernacle valued the "new song," spontaneity, intercessory worship, and a Spirit-led atmosphere where God could speak and move. These musicians and singers were not just singing rote songs to fill the time slots and do their duty. They were connecting deeply to the heart of God and learning to flow with the Spirit of God. This enabled the Levites to tap into God's desires for Israel and the other nations of the earth. The intimate worship produced an overflowing spirit of intercession and prayer. As they aligned their songs with heaven, they came into agreement with God's purposes for the earth.

Over fifty Psalms serve as prophecies of Jesus, the Messiah. The Davidic worshipers received incredibly accurate and detailed revelations regarding Jesus's birth, ministry, death, resurrection, and second coming. Imagine prophesying via songs with pinpoint accuracy about events that would happen 1,000 years later! Jesus Himself quotes one of David's psalms while hanging on the cross (Psalm 22:1). While there is no indication David appointed intercessors in the tabernacle, the musicians and singers were intercessory worshipers whose songs became prophecies and prayers for God's kingdom purposes. They prayed for the peace of their city (Psalm 122:6-7). They realized that their prayers rose to God like incense (Psalm 141:2). Davidic worship was "intercessory worship."

David Fritch points out the common thread between praise, thanksgiving, intercession, and prophecy is *agreement*. Praise is agreement with God's nature. Thanksgiving is agreement with what God has done. Intercession is agreement with God's will. And prophecy is agreement with what God is going to do.[6] Whether praise, prayer and prophecy, the songs at David's tabernacle were all about agreement with God. This agreement

---

6   Fritch, *Enthroned*, 54-55.

with heaven created a powerful atmosphere where God's presence and power could manifest in Israel, and it would ripple into the millennia to come.

Meditation on God's Word

While there was a heavy emphasis on prophetic songs and the moving of God's Holy Spirit at the tent, there was also a deep rootedness in the Torah. In the midst of the day-and-night prophetic songs in David's tabernacle there was day-and-night meditation on God's Word. One of the very first verses of the Psalms highlights this value. It begins by contrasting those who are foolish with the wise who meditate on the Scriptures "day and night" (Psalm 1:2).

David's value for God's Word/Law is apparent throughout the Psalms. In fact, the longest Psalm in the Bible, chapter 119, is primarily focused on receiving revelation from God's Law. He declares that God's Word is his "meditation all the day" (Ps. 119:97), and says to the Lord, "Your statutes have been my songs" (Ps. 119:54). One could envision David's tabernacle as a "singing seminary" where Israel grew in revelation, sound theology, and the knowledge of God.

The unique combination of a prophetic atmosphere coupled with a high value for God's Word in David's Tabernacle is similar to those in the church at Antioch, who hosted both teachers and prophets as they ministered to God (Acts 13:1-3). The New Testament likewise instructs us to let God's Word dwell in us richly as we sing (Colossians 3:16) and to be filled with the Holy Spirit when we sing (Ephesians 5:19). This blend of the Spirit of God and the Word of God also reminds us of Jesus' teaching that true worshipers worship in both "spirit" and "truth" (John 4:23). The praise at David's tabernacle embraced this glorious tension.

Antiphonal Singing

One facet of Davidic worship is antiphonal singing, demonstrated clearly in the revivals under the leadership of Nehemiah and Ezra, when they restored worship according to David's original tabernacle.[7] The Levitical singers were established in teams that ministered to God together in an antiphonal way, with singers responding back and forth. The Bible describes "two large choirs" (Nehemiah 12:31, 38) that stood on opposite sides of the wall to sing, and it later mentions some of the Levites "who stood opposite them to praise" (Nehemiah 12:24). In Ezra it says that the Levites "sang responsively" "according to the directions of David" (Ezra 3:11).

In other words, one group of singers would stand on one side while another choir stood on the opposite side. They would go back and forth "responsively" or "antiphonally" in short bursts of song. All of this was happening while flowing with the Holy Spirit in prophetic worship! It's fascinating how these "liturgical" and

God's glory was resting on their nation. Nothing like this had ever happened before.

"charismatic" elements of worship were united in the Davidic worship model. The values of team ministry, structure, Spirit-led flow, and unity were all present. Psalm 136 is an example of what the antiphonal singing could have looked like in David's day. The psalm contains twenty-six unique lines, each followed by the phrase "for his steadfast love endures forever." One could imagine one of the choirs singing the phrases with the other choir echoing the response.

Responsive singing reflects the heavenly throne room scene in Revelation 5 where elders, living creatures, and angels respond

---

7   As we will study more later, each revival in Israel's history corresponds with a resurgence of the Davidic order of worship.

back-and-forth with praise and worship. The four living creatures and twenty-four elders launch the song with a "Worthy" verse (verses 8-10). The multitude of angels respond with an abbreviated "Worthy" refrain (verses 11-12), and then the multitude of saints repeat the final phases of the angel's chorus (verse 13). Finally, the four living creatures add an "Amen" to the whole song (verse 14). Certainly David's tabernacle was reflecting a measure of the heavenly antiphony where every tribe, tongue, and nation are joined with the angelic hosts in day-and-night worship.

The Fruit of David's Tabernacle

David reigned in Jerusalem for thirty-three years (1 Kings 2:11), and it appears that his tabernacle of worship continued with limited interruption throughout that time.[8] David's reign in Jerusalem is considered by many as the high point of Israel's history, and his era was the last time that all twelve tribes of Israel would be in unity.[9]

David uniquely gathered "all Israel together" to bring the ark of the covenant and establish the worship tent (1 Chronicles 13:5, 15:3). He mobilized "all the leaders of Israel" (1 Chronicles 28:1) to unite in funding the day-and-night worship (1 Chronicles 29:1-9) before passing off the kingdom to his son, Solomon. While David experienced many personal challenges as king,[10] the nation

---

8 The one exception seems to be during Absalom's rebellion when the ark of the covenant was briefly taken out of Jerusalem in 2 Samuel 15:24-29.

9 "The reigns of David and Solomon formed the high-water mark of Israel's prosperity, as the time when the whole nation was unified and had one King..." see A.G. Herbert, *The Throne of David* (7th impression. London: Faber and Faber Limited, 1956), 41. He later says of Israel that "They look back to the reign of David as the ideal time, and they long—how they long—for it to return," page 42.

10 The book of 1 Chronicles seems to underscore David's struggles, while the book of 2 Samuel is more willing to expose David's flaws and failures.

also experienced many victories in battle (1 Chronicles 14:16-17, 2 Samuel 7:1), and justice was established in the land (2 Samuel 8:15) during his reign.

The Scriptures paint a vivid picture of the incredible worship at David's historic tent and its impact on the nation of Israel. God's manifest presence was central and accessible. The Levites were singing, playing instruments, dancing, shouting, and celebrating. The Spirit of God was flowing with revelation as they sang the "new songs" of praise, prophecy, and the Word of God. Multi-generational teams of worshipers were being trained with excellence and creativity. Choirs were assembled. New instruments were created. Resources were allocated to finance the whole project. God's glory was resting on their nation. Nothing like this had ever happened before.

And all of this was happening non-stop—twenty-four seven—day and night—for thirty-three years!

So he left Asaph and his relatives there before the ark of the covenant of the Lord, to minister before the ark continually, as every day's work required (1 Chronicles 16:37, NASB).

Why on earth would David require the Levites to keep the songs going non-stop? Why would the musicians and singers have to stand outside, in the middle of the night, to praise the Lord and pray? We will take the entire next chapter to explore the "day-and-night" nature of Davidic worship.

- We come boldly — minister to his presence in the throne room.
- Centered around music/musicians.

Heb 13:5

- Equipping / Training up.
  Mentoring / discipleship.

- Excellence not perfect.

- Heartfelt.

- Intercessory

- Prophetic
  Not trained just to praise but
  ~~prophesy~~ prophecy.

we are prophetic worshipers

Practice :- sing the word each day.
Zeph 3 : 17
He is singing a song in heaven.

The Fire on the Altar

Within the first year after we launched our 6:22 youth worship ministry, a leader at our church heard some teachings on the Tabernacle of David. He had the idea of hosting twenty-four hours of non-stop worship at our church. He invited worship leaders from various churches to take slots and cover the entire time. Since we already hosted our 6:22 meetings on Friday nights, we kicked off that first "Twenty-four Hour Worship" event in the spring of 2003. This was our first taste of any kind of "day and night" worship, and we would go on to host these annually for many years. By 2007, we had increased the frequency of these twenty-four-hour worship gatherings to every month.

What I would discover was that our little community in eastern North Carolina was not the only one beginning to experiment with day and night worship and prayer. An unprecedented global prayer movement, fueled with musical worship, was spreading around the world. The story of David's tabernacle was inspiring a multitude of communities, churches, and movements who were organizing expressions of 24/7 prayer and worship. In my early twenties, I found myself discovering this day and night prayer and worship movement, and I was intrigued and invigorated by this vision of unceasing worship and prayer.

Houses of Prayer

During the years we were hosting twenty-four-hour worship weekends, my friends and I would go to Morningstar Church in Charlotte for their conferences, which were marked by a hunger for God's presence, prophetic ministry, creative worship, and freedom. One time while visiting, we heard that there was a twenty-four-hour prayer room that had been set up on the same campus as the church. It was called Zadok House of Prayer (ZHOP). Dozens of missionaries from Kansas City had moved to Charlotte to establish 24/7 prayer with live worship.

I remember going to visit ZHOP the first time between sessions at a Morningstar conference. I walked into a relatively small room with a few musicians and singers in the corner. There was "prophetic artwork" on the walls and on easels. A few people sat on the chairs with their Bibles. They were singing some soft, devotional worship music. Shortly after arriving, the tone of the meeting shifted. Someone got on the microphone to announce that they would be praying for a team in Washington DC that was working for the pro-life cause. The team began to rumble with a flurry of passionate intercessory prayers, Scripture reading, and singing. They would bounce back and forth between someone's spoken prayers and singing the prayers. They used phrases from Scripture to create their spontaneous prayer songs. And God's presence filled the room in a powerful way as everyone crescendoed in a united song of intercession. The music increased dynamically, but so did the activity of the Holy Spirit. I felt myself getting lost in the flow of the music, the Word of God, and the prayer.

Suddenly I realized it had been over an hour. Had I been praying for an hour? And enjoying it? I didn't really like prayer that much. I loved music and worship, but I found it hard to pray. But something about what they did at ZHOP made prayer more fun. I later found out they were using a prayer model called "Harp & Bowl" that was developed at the International House of Prayer in Kansas City (IHOP-KC).

There was something very "Davidic" about the worship at Morningstar. They were prophetic. They were creative and excellent at their musical craft. The manifest presence of God was palpable at their gatherings. They loved God's Word. These values were already influencing our local ministry. But there was also something "Davidic" about ZHOP. Most notably, the song never stopped, just like David's Tabernacle. The flow of antiphonal, intercessory worship also seemed to line up with the descriptions of the worship at David's tent. Many of the musicians and singers were even full-time staff—like modern-day Levites. It was almost like ZHOP was a mini, indoor "David's tabernacle." As I continued to visit Charlotte, I would find myself sneaking away from the large conference sessions to go to the prayer room to worship and pray with a handful of folks who were maintaining that continuous flame of non-stop musical prayer.

Naturally, I discovered more about the ZHOP "mothership" in Kansas City. The International House of Prayer (IHOP-KC) was launched by Mike Bickle in 1999. Their missions base has been hosting 24/7, non-stop prayer with live worship since September of that year. Before launching IHOP, their local church in Kansas City was a thriving young adult church with a culture of prayer. Bickle's congregation had been hosting three daily prayer meetings since the early 1980s. God began to supernaturally lead them to launch IHOP-KC in May of 1999, and they expanded to a full 24/7 schedule by that fall. Some of their church staff and young adults quit their jobs to become "intercessory missionaries" with IHOP-KC and help Bickle launch the non-stop prayer room. At the time of writing, they have had over twenty million man-hours of prayer and over 20,000 full-time staff (present and former) serving at their missions base. Mike Bickle has hours of recordings on their website that share the story and prophetic history of their ministry and movement. It's fascinating.[1] As of 2017, Bickle estimated that there were around 20,000 "houses of prayer" around the world that are utilizing a ministry model similar to IHOP-KC.[2]

Another 24-7 Prayer Movement

Around the time I discovered this day and night "house of prayer" movement, I saw a copy of a magazine with a guy named Pete Greig on the cover. I was shocked to discover he was also doing something called "24-7 Prayer" in the United Kingdom. I was stirred by his story (and especially his poem titled "The Vision"), so I ordered his book to learn more about their ministry.

As a young church leader, Pete wanted something to help kickstart spiritual awakening at their local church. He had heard the story of the Moravians in Herrnhut, Germany in the eighteenth century. These Moravians were living in a community started by Count Ludwig von Zinzendorf. After an outpouring of God's Spirit during communion one evening in the summer of 1727, they collectively launched a 24/7 prayer watch that lasted over 100 years. In teams of two they would take shifts at their chapel to pray. The overflow of their life of prayer was a profound missionary zeal. Their small community sent out over 200 missionaries in the following decades. The Moravian missionaries' passion for Jesus and peace in the midst of crisis is what brought about John Wesley's conversion to Christ. The Moravians also influenced William Carey, who is considered the

---

1   https://www.ihopkc.org/prophetichistory/
2   https://jerryjohnston.com/jerry-johnston-interviews-mike-bickle-of-ihop-young-people-want-something-to-die-for/

"father of modern missions." Their global impact was birthed in a small community that was committed to following Christ and praying together day and night.

Pete Greig thought that if it worked for Moravians, perhaps it would work for their young church. So they decided to try one week of 24/7 prayer at their youth church in England (this was also in 1999). As a creative community, they decorated a room with interactive "prayer stations" and a variety of music options so that people could take their personal prayer shifts to fill the week of prayer. Not only did God move powerfully within their congregation, but unbelievers visited the prayer room to experience God's presence. Many decided to follow Jesus. As reports of miracles and salvation spread, believers from other churches and cities came to visit as well. Unbeknownst to Pete, these other churches started hosting their own 24/7 prayer rooms in their churches. Then they started calling and emailing him about how to do it, and the 24-7 Prayer movement was accidentally born. At the time of this writing, the 24-7 Prayer website states that they have tracked over 20,000 prayer rooms that have hosted a week or more of 24/7 prayer. At their fifteen-year anniversary, they mentioned that those prayer rooms had been hosted in over 125 nations around the world.[3]

What Was Happening in 1999?

In the UK, nobody wanted to stop after Pete Greig's week of prayer, so they continued for months. A few weeks later, across the pond, Mike Bickle's team launched their 24/7 prayer with live worship in Kansas City. On the very same night that IHOP-KC went 24/7, Every Home For Christ was breaking ground on a 24/7 prayer center in Colorado Springs (I will share more about

---

3   Pete Greig and Dave Roberts, *Red Moon Rising: Rediscover the Power of Prayer* (Colorado Springs, CO: Navpress, 2015), 74-77.

this in a moment). And astonishingly none of them were aware of the others!

- September 5, 1999—Pete Greig's team launches a week of 24/7 prayer [4]
- September 19, 1999—International House of Prayer goes 24/7[5]
- September 19, 1999—24/7 Jericho Prayer Center breaks ground in Colorado Springs[6]

It is safe to say that IHOP-KC and 24-7 Prayer have now "gone viral" and impacted the body of Christ at large. Even more astounding is that other groups around the world have felt prompted by the Lord to host prayer rooms or extended hours of Davidic worship while being totally unaware of groups like IHOP-KC or 24-7 Prayer. There is clearly a profound move of the Holy Spirit of God in our day! The "spirit of the tabernacle of David" is emerging in the church of the nations. This "global prayer movement" is not rooted in any one ministry or organization. I am convinced that God Himself is orchestrating

Why were so many historic prayer and worship movements begun at the same time? God was birthing a global day-and-night prayer movement that will lead to a historic harvest of souls entering the kingdom.

the greatest movement of worship and prayer in Christian history. And it's happening day and night around the world!

It was also 1999 when Lou Engle birthed "The Call," which

---

4   https://www.24-7prayer.com/blog/2828/pete-greig-on-20year-sof247

5   https://www.ihopkc.org/prophetichistory/

6   https://lovesmessenger.net/convergence-of-missions-and-prayer-ihop-kcs-role-to-serve-others/

was a massive mobilizer of prayer and fasting in the early twenty-first century. The Call hosted a number of "solemn assemblies" of united fasting and prayer based on Joel 2. At the first Call event, over 400,000 gathered on the National Mall in Washington DC on September 2, 2000.

What was happening at the turn of the century? Why were so many historic prayer and worship movements begun at the same time? Engle believes that God was birthing a global day and night prayer movement that would lead to a historic harvest of souls entering the kingdom.[7] Here is Stephen Venable's perspective on the explosive growth of day-and-night prayer and worship:

The recent trend of massive gatherings for worship, fasting and prayer occurring in stadiums across the earth is surely one of the most visible evidences of this movement, but just as important is the marked increase of small meetings at local churches. Within the larger contours of the international prayer movement is the phenomenon of houses of prayer.

---

7 He says: "In 1994, Bill Bright, founder of Campus Crusade for Christ, felt stirred to call a corporate 40-Day Fast for the whole nation. He was 'impressed by the Spirit to pray that two million believers [would] humble themselves by seeking God in forty-day fasts.' The promise from God was the following: 'America and the rest of the world will before the end of the year 2000 experience a great spiritual awakening! And this revival will spark the greatest spiritual harvest in the history of the Church.' As a response, Bright gathered 600 major leaders from across ministries and denominations later that winter in Orlando to share the vision and launch the fast. Many leaders in the Body of Christ, including Billy Graham, endorsed this call to fast. Myself and others went on extended seasons of fasting and prayer, believing that this was a true word from God. Some estimate that hundreds of thousands, if not millions, went on forty-day fasts in that season. Many would ask, 'Where is the harvest?' because they equate great spiritual awakening with the harvest. But look again at what Bright predicted. His actual word was that awakening would lead to harvest. I believe a remarkable spiritual awakening did indeed begin before the year 2000 in the form of a global prayer movement." _https://thejesusfast.global/harvest-is-coming/

> *Without any united effort or centralized organization what-soever, Christians all across the earth are gathering with a common longing to establish night and day prayer in their cities and regions. It must be emphasized that this has never happened before.*[8]

This has never happened before.

As we will study further, David's tabernacle pioneered the first known initiative of 24/7 worship and prayer on the earth. But something much bigger is happening in our day that is spreading like wildfire. It's not just one city or one nation. There is a global worship and prayer movement that is fueling the greatest missions movement the world has ever seen.

The Prayer Corps & The Jericho Center

On September 19, 1999, the same day that IHOP was shifting into a 24/7 schedule in Kansas City, Dick Eastman was breaking ground on the Jericho Center in Colorado Springs, CO. The Jericho Center was being dedicated as a place for—you guessed it—24/7 prayer! Dick Eastman was the director of Every Home for Christ, a global missions organization focused on sharing the Gospel door-to-door around the world. Their missionaries and volunteers strategically blanket certain cities with prayer and evangelism.

Dick is an influential leader in the Christian missions movement, but he is a worshiper and intercessor at heart. He has written extensively on the power of worship and prayer, especially as it relates to its impact on the effectiveness of evangelism and missions.[9] During the Jesus People movement, Dick helped organize what is probably one of the first expressions of 24/7

---

8   http://www.beholdingjesus.com/wp-content/uploads/2011/09/BFNDWP_SUM10_S01_Perspective.doc.

9   Most notably his book *Intercessory Worship*.

prayer and worship in America.[10] It was called the "Prayer Corps" and was launched after Dick Eastman had a vision on Thanksgiving Day 1971 of a youth revival fueled by 24/7 prayer.[11]

God used their 24/7 "prayer corps" ministry powerfully in California during the hippie movement. So when Dick became president of Every Home for Christ, he wanted to establish strategic 24/7 prayer and worship to fuel their international missions ministry. That is what motivated the launch of their Jericho Center in Colorado Springs, which exists to facilitate day-and-night prayer. Since initiating such prayer at the Jericho Center, Every Home for Christ has doubled the reported number of salvations in the nations through their movement![12]

The Incessant Flame

Nearly all of these "24/7" groups have looked to David's tabernacle as a biblical source of inspiration for their day-and-night prayer.[13] The idea of 24/7 prayer and David's tabernacle are now inextricably linked in the hearts and minds of a generation.

---

10   I must credit the longest known day & night prayer & worship meeting in the United States. The Fransiscan Sisters of Perpetual Adoration in Wisconsin hosted corporate 24/7 adoration and prayer with at least two people from August 1, 1878 until Feb. 25, 2020. See https://www.fspa.org/content/prayer/perpetual-adoration/

11   See his book *The Purple Pig*.

12   https://prayerhub.org/prayer-news/item/8776-every-home-for-christ-and-jericho-center-the-amazing-multiplication-of-ministry-impact-through-strategic-targeted-praying

13   It's worth noting that some question if the worship at David's tabernacle was literally 24/7/365. For instance, Mike Bickle states in *Growing in Prayer*, page 217: "The Scripture makes it clear that the Levites ministered to God 'night and day' and that there was a special blessing for those who praise the Lord in the night. Many people believe that Davidic worship was 24/7, however, there is no clear statement in the Scripture that proves beyond doubt that David's order of worship was continual in the sense of ongoing worship twenty-four hours a day. We know for sure that it was continual in the sense of night and day."

One of the historic stories that has inspired nearly all these movements is that of the Moravian community in Germany. Their legacy has provoked many of the modern-day expressions of day-and-night worship and prayer. Interestingly, the Moravians also included songs in their 24/7 prayer watch.

> On August 26th twenty-four Brethren and the same number of Sisters met, and covenanted together to continue from one midnight to the next in prayer, dividing for that purpose the twentyfour hours of night and day by lot among themselves.... August 27th this new regulation was put into practice.... the resolution was taken that if anyone could not spend the whole hour in prayer, either because of indigence of spirit or official concerns preventing him, *he might sing spiritual songs and hymns of praise to the Lord,* and thus bring unto Him, for himself and his fellow Brethren, either the sacrifice of thanksgiving or the offering of prayer and supplication.[14]

In a sense, the Moravians were quite *Davidic* in their approach to 24/7. Just as David's Levites offered 24/7 "intercessory praise and worship," the Moravians seemed to have also offered 24/7 "praise and prayer." The Moravians based their 24/7 prayer watch on a verse from Moses's tabernacle about the altar of incense. Leviticus 6:13 says, *"Fire shall be kept burning on the altar continually; it shall not go out."* Israel's Levitical community was familiar with maintaining their priestly duties continuously. The altar in Moses's tabernacle burned incessantly, and the Levites were responsible to keep that fire burning and guard the tabernacle through the night hours. There was always someone on guard at Moses's tabernacle at any given moment. When the Levites transitioned to Jerusalem, they would have simply continued their normal routines of non-

---

14   *The Memorial Days of the Renewed Church of the Brethren,* 138. (Emphasis mine.)

stop ministry, albeit with a new expression — the fire that would be maintained would be the flame of worship and prayer.

Commentators agree that the perpetual fire on the altar of the Mosaic tabernacle points to perpetual prayer and worship. Matthew Henry writes, *"Thus should the fire of our holy affections, the exercise of our faith and love, of prayer and praise, be without ceasing."*[15] Peter Leithart compares the "watches" that the singers took at David's tabernacle to the *"guard duty of priests and Levites at the Mosaic tabernacle.... Musical performance is described under the metaphor of guard duty."* [16] Just as Moses's tabernacle was guarded constantly, the ark of the covenant was to be "guarded" with the ongoing praise of the Levites at David's tabernacle. This day and night "watch" sounds similar to the intercessory watchmen described by the prophet Isaiah.

> I have set watchmen on your walls, O Jerusalem; they shall never hold their peace day or night. You who make mention of the Lord, do not keep silent, And give Him no rest till He establishes And till He makes Jerusalem a praise in the earth (Isaiah 62:6-7).

This incredible prophecy from Isaiah speaks about 24/7 communities that God will raise up in the days preceding the return of Jesus. These communities are described as "watchmen on the wall." In ancient history, the walled cities would be wide enough that guards could stand on the wall to keep a lookout for invaders or visitors. To keep a city safe, it was required that a watchman always be on duty—even throughout the night. Isaiah is describing prophetic intercessors like watchmen on the walls

---

15   Matthew Henry, "Leviticus 6," in *Matthew Henry's Commentary on the Whole Bible* (Posted on Bible Hub. https://biblehub.com/com mentaries/mhcw/leviticus/6.htm).

16   Leithart, *From Silence to Song*, 65.

of a city. The prayers and worship of these watchmen will rise to God day and night across the earth before Christ returns. I believe Jesus himself is recalling this prophecy when He invites the church to "cry out day and night" to God for justice before He comes again (Luke 18:7-8).

Day and Night Songs

Throughout the Scriptures the phrase "day and night" is a way of saying "all the time." The passage from Isaiah 62:6-7 above is a clear indication of this. Those who are "never" silent are calling on the Lord "day and night." They give themselves "no rest." Isaiah 60:11 describes the gates of the new Jerusalem being open "day and night." Yet a few verses later it says, "Your sun shall no more go down, nor your moon withdraw itself; for the Lord will be your everlasting light" (verse 20). How can the gates be open "day and night" if there is no day or night!? It is abundantly clear that the gates being open day and night means that the gates of the new Jerusalem are *always* open. Likewise, the musicians and singers in David's tabernacle are described as serving in their ministry day and night.

> *Now these, the singers, the heads of fathers' houses of the Levites, were in the chambers of the temple free from other service, for they were <u>on duty day and night</u> (1 Chronicles 9:33).*

Matthew Henry sees 1 Chronicles 9:33 as evidence of constant singing. He says, *"It should seem, some companies were continually singing, at least at stated hours, both day and night. Thus was God continually praised, as it is fit he should be who is continually doing good."* The Psalms describe David and others pursuing God's presence "day and night" (Psalm 1:2, 88:1) and specifically in the tabernacle's "night watches" (Psalm 63:6, 119:148). Psalm 134 is a short chapter dedicated entirely to the Levites who were specifically assigned to offering Davidic worship during the watches of the night hours.

Behold, bless the Lord, All you servants of the Lord, Who by night stand in the house of the Lord! Lift up your hands to the holy place and bless the Lord. May the Lord bless you from Zion, he who made heaven and earth! (Psalm 134).

There is a special blessing designated for those who are committed to these night hours of ministry to the Lord. The Levites were literally staying up into the late night or early morning hours, and it explains why there is a special psalm dedicated to those making this unique sacrifice. These Levites were working third shift, and if you have ever tried to stay up praying and worshiping all night long, then you understand both the special challenges and blessings of this kind of ministry! Commentator Albert Barnes says of Psalm 134:

The Levites worshiped continuously at David's tabernacle on Mount Zion as they hosted the presence of God night and day. David would not let the fire on the altar go out.

There was a class of singers in the temple who devoted the night… to praise; and it is possible that this service may have been, as it was subsequently in some of the monasteries, continued by succeeding choirs, during the entire night.[17]

The monasteries and choirs Barnes describes are those such as the one started by Alexander Akimetes near the Euphrates river around AD 400. Monks were organized into choirs who

17   Barnes, Albert. "Psalms 134" in *Albert Barnes' Notres on the Whole Bible* (Posted on Studylight.org. https://www.studylight.org/commentaries/eng/bnb/psalms-134.html)

rotated to sing 24/7 for twenty years. They called this ministry *laus perennis,* which is the Latin phrase for perpetual prayer. Some described these zealous monks as the *Acoemetae,* which means the "sleepless ones." Other similar monasteries were established throughout the Middle Ages.[18] I wonder if they were inspired by the day and night, Davidic choirs of Nehemiah's day that we described in the last chapter?[19]

The Stretch to Day and Night

David's tabernacle was clearly a *day-and-night* institution. The Levites are also described in 1 Chronicles 16:37 as offering their praise to God "continually" before the ark of the covenant. The Hebrew word for "continually" here means "stretching...constant...continual...perpetual."[20]

There is a special blessing designated for those who are committed to the night hours of ministry to the Lord.

The root of tamiyd means "to stretch." I believe this is the heart of day-and-night worship and prayer. It is not about filling slots in a 24/7 schedule or doing the bare minimum to keep things going. It is about stretching towards extravagant worship. It's about more. It's about longer. It's about continuation. It's about the process and the journey and the growth and the reach. 24/7 worship and prayer is not a prize at the end of the tunnel. 24/7 is not the magic key that will release revival. Expressions of day-and-night worship are a response to those who have seen Jesus and collec-

18   Mike Bickle, *Growing in Prayer: A Real-Life Guide to Talking With God* (Lake Mary, FL: Charisma House, 2014), 243-245.
19   Nehemiah 12:31,38.
20   "H8548," *The Strongest Strong's Exhaustive Concordance of the Bible.* Grand Rapids, MI: Zondervan, 2001.

tively stretch themselves to respond in proportion to His worth.

Our hearts need to stretch to receive fresh revelation that incites a fresh response. As our hearts stretch, our outward response needs to stretch. Our schedules need to stretch to make more time for Him. What if we stayed a little longer? It's not about filling worship slots and sets. It's about lingering in His presence. Let's stretch it out. I say that we "tamiyd" our worship and prayer times, even if we can't go 24/7. The first song sang at David's Tabernacle used this word "tamiyd." Asaph sang: "Seek the Lord and his strength, seek his face continually [tamiyd]" (1 Chronicles 16:11).

It's not about the arrival. It's about the seeking. The stretching. Day and night.

The same word, tamiyd, is used in other Scripture passages to clearly indicate something that is going non-stop (see Exodus 25:30, Numbers 9:16, and Isaiah 21:8, 49:16). Dick Eastman points out that the word is also used to describe the perpetual cloud of God's presence that filled the Mosaic tabernacle.[21] Just as God's glory rested continuously at Moses's tabernacle, the Levites worshiped God continuously at David's tabernacle on Mount Zion as they hosted the presence of God with their prophetic songs night and day. David would not let the fire on the altar go out. And this same passion for extravagant worship and prayer is arising in our day—not just in one place, but around the world.

---

21   Dick Eastman, *Intercessory Worship: Combining Worship & Prayer to Touch the Heart of God* (Grand Rapids, MI: Chosen Books, 2011), 118.

A Place for God

*I will not give sleep to my eyes or slumber to my eyelids, until I
find a place for the Lord, a dwelling place for the Mighty One
of Jacob (Psalm 132:4-5).*

After several years of hosting worship and prayer gatherings, we
began to be gripped by this idea of a place of ongoing worship
and prayer. Our Friday worship nights had continued, but other
expressions of prayer and worship were also emerging in our city.
By 2007, we began hosting twenty-four-hour worship weekends
almost every month. In 2008, a local church had hosted ten
months of 24-7 prayer in their sanctuary. Around the same time,
campus ministries at East Carolina University started hosting
weeks of 24-7 prayer, as well as late-night worship and prayer
gatherings during the week. Many of us were longing for a place
to host God's presence in an ongoing way in our region, much like
David longed for a place for God's presence. Up to that point,
local churches had always let us utilize their facilities, but what
would it look like for our community to have a dedicated place for
worship and prayer? A place for God?

During that season, I would go around and visit prayer
meetings in our city. A local intercessor named Nancy attended
one of these meetings, and she was one of those special "prayer

warriors" who seemed to have a direct line to God. When she prayed for stuff, stuff happened! After a prayer meeting in early 2009, Nancy came to me unprovoked and said, "So when are you getting a building for your ministry?"

What she didn't know was that my wife and I had recently been driving around Greenville looking at buildings, dreaming about a place for a house of worship and prayer—a "tabernacle of David" for our city. You have to understand: We were newlyweds with no money. No resources. No plan. We were just dreaming and praying together!

A Boiler Room

While roaming the city, we had found an abandoned hotel with a conference center that we thought was really cool. We circled the facility, looking for a sign somewhere that would indicate who might own the property. The only sign we found was on a door on the back of the building that read "Boiler Room." We were so excited, because we had heard about the 24-7 Prayer movement in the United Kingdom calling their prayer rooms "boiler rooms." The term "boiler room" was borrowed from Charles Spurgeon, who used to attribute the success of his preaching to his "boiler rooms"—his rooms of intercessors that he considered the power source of his ministry. We thought the sign on the hotel must be a sign from God. We were sure this meant that God was going to give us that building as a "boiler room" for our city! We could house the homeless, establish 24-7 worship and prayer, host conference events, and more. It would be an amazing ministry center to impact our region.

Within a few weeks, the building had been demolished. Bulldozed to the ground. We were dumbfounded. So, we drove around the city again, looking and dreaming. We saw a smaller space for rent in the heart of downtown Greenville. It was above a skateboard shop on a corner. Across the street was East Carolina University. The opposite direction was the main downtown strip of bars, clubs, and restaurants where ECU students would come to party on the weekends. It was much smaller. The aesthetic was raw and grungy. But the location was amazing. It was a few weeks after all this that Nancy asked me about a building. I told her that we were dreaming together, and she asked if we had a location in mind. I told her about the building downtown above the skate shop. She said she would start praying.

Within a few months, I had shared the whole story with our ministry's board of directors. We ended up driving downtown to see the space for rent. In the parking lot, one of our board members, a local dentist, randomly started weeping. He said he had just heard the audible voice of God say, "This is a place I want my glory to dwell." We were stunned.

He then told us God was leading him to rent the building for us. I suggested that we should probably look inside and find out how much it cost first! He was not deterred. Regardless of the details, he said that God had spoken. He was committed to rent that space for us in order to obey God's voice and establish a place of worship and prayer in downtown Greenville. We ended up calling it the Boiler Room.[1]

Thin Places

It was clear that God was asking us to host His presence in

---

1 The Boiler Room served as a house of prayer missions base in Greenville, NC from 2009 to 2016, when God led us to move out of that building after exactly seven years. We hosted over 7000 hours of live worship and prayer there, and many people were saved, healed, refreshed, trained and sent out during that time. We have a Boiler Room archive w/photos, videos, and music available at prayforgreenville.org.

a specific place. Like David prepared a tent on Mount Zion for the ark of the covenant, we were preparing a place for day-and-night worship and prayer in our city. We always knew that the building itself wasn't really the "place" for God; that has always been His people. The Scriptures say that we are living stones built together as a house for the Lord (I Peter 2:5). We are the spiritual "place" where God dwells on the earth (Ephesians 2:21-22). But apparently, He also wanted a specific geographic area to assemble His living stones.

We had read about what the monks called "thin places"—places where they said that the veil between heaven and earth became thin. Some charismatic folks use the word "portals" to describe these geographic locations where God seems to uniquely manifest His glory. It just seems that in some areas it is easier to be aware of God's manifest presence. Pete Greig explains:

> We are told that, prior to giving the Lord's Prayer, "Jesus was praying in a certain place." That's significant. There seem to have been certain places in which he preferred to pray. Elsewhere, he advised his disciples, "When you pray, go into your room, close the door." The location clearly mattered. On the day of Pentecost, we are told that the Holy Spirit first "filled the whole house where they were sitting" so that the disciples "saw what seemed to be tongues of fire" and then, moments later, "all of them were filled with the Holy Spirit." Isn't that an interesting progression? The Holy Spirit filled the place before he filled the people.[2]

I don't totally understand this phenomenon, but I think about the story of Elisha's bones. Even though Elisha was dead,

---

2   Pete Greig, *How to Pray: A Simple Guide for Normal People* (Colorado Springs, CO: Navpress, 2019), 9-10.

those who touched his bones were resurrected (2 Kings 13:21). It was like a residue of God's presence was resting on a physical place. My theory is that if there is a place on earth where God is welcomed consistently, it becomes a "thin place" where His manifest presence seems to linger, even after we leave.

Why Jerusalem?

In Psalm 132, we discover that God was inviting David to establish a thin place in Jerusalem, also known as Mt. Zion: *"For the Lord has chosen Zion; He has desired it for His dwelling place"* (Ps. 132:5). God said that Jerusalem was to be the resting place for the ark of the covenant. Bible teachers have various theories about why David chose Jerusalem to be the new capital of Israel. Many believe it was because the geography of the region was beneficial to providing water, or that the

We are the spiritual "place" where God dwells on the earth. But apparently, He also wanted a specific geographic area to assemble His living stones.

hills protected them from invaders. But I wonder if there is a more spiritual reason?

The first time we see Jerusalem mentioned in Scripture is in a strange story with Abraham and a character named Melchizedek. It says in Genesis 14:18:

> *Then Melchizedek **king** of Salem brought out bread and wine; he was the **priest** of God Most High.*

The Salem where Melchizedek was king would become known as Jeru*salem*. This king Melchizedek was also a priest of Yahweh on Mt Zion, and he brought out bread and wine to give to Abraham after a battle. Over 500 years before David became king, God was already being worshiped and ministered to by a priest (who was a king) in this same place. We will learn more about Melchizedek later, but it makes me wonder if God's desire to dwell on Mt Zion had something to do with this priest-king. I wonder if Zion was already a thin place before David got there? Either way, Jerusalem was God's place. It was there that David would establish his tabernacle—the "boiler room" of Israel. Like our little prayer room in Greenville, David's tabernacle was a simple structure marked by God's glorious presence and power.

The Manifest Presence of God

It was probably David's son Solomon who was inspired to write Psalm 132 in remembrance of his father. The song begins with David's afflictions, but it is primarily about David's vision for a dwelling place of God's presence and the vow that he made before God to see that vision come to pass. David's longing for God grew into a burning desire to establish a resting place for the manifest presence of God on the earth. As king of Israel, David wanted his kingdom to experience that presence. This is what led to the great procession of the ark and gave birth to David's tabernacle.

I will not give sleep to my eyes or slumber to my eyelids, until I find a place for the Lord, a dwelling place for the Mighty One of Jacob (Psalm 132:4-5).

To understand David's vision for a dwelling place for God, we need to understand the different dimensions of God's presence described in the Scriptures. There is a genuine, biblical understanding that God is everywhere. This is called God's omnipresence. David was well aware of this dimension of God's presence. He knew he could never get away from the watchful eye of the Lord (Psalm 139:7-8). No one can hide from God. AW Tozer says of God's omnipresence: *"In His infinitude He surrounds the finite creation and contains it. There is no place beyond Him for anything to be."*[3]

But this is not what we mean when we typically refer to God's presence. Even though He is everywhere, we may not recognize or sense Him. When we speak of God's presence, we typically mean His manifest presence, which is where God makes His omnipresence known to people in a particular place. Jack Hayford describes this as:

> **"...invading circumstances, moving in power, demonstrating His grace, revealing His sovereign might, extending His kingdom mercies and transforming people, churches, communities and whole regions of the earth."**[4]

What Hayford writes is what David had in mind when he made his vow in Psalm 132. His vision was that God would make Himself known in his life, in his city, and in his nation. Jesus spoke of God's manifest presence when He promised to be among His followers when two or three gather together in His name (Matthew 18:20). Jesus is already everywhere, but his promise to be "in the midst" of his disciples indicates that we can experience a particular *manifestation* of His presence. David's "dwelling place" vision was for God's *manifest presence* to fill the nation of Israel, where people would be experiencing a strong sense of God's glory, nearness, and power. His idea was that God's glory and presence would rest in a particular geographic place. For David that place was Jerusalem. *"For the Lord has chosen Zion; He has desired it for His dwelling place"* (Ps. 132:13).

Some might argue that we already have God's presence with us because Christians have the Holy Spirit inside them. Yes! As

3   A.W. Tozer, *The Knowledge of the Holy* (New York: HarperCollins, 1964), 74.
4   Jack Hayford, *The Reward of Worship: The Joy of Fellowship with a Personal God* (Grand Rapids, MI: Chosen Books, 2005), 23.

Christians, we receive the Holy Spirit at the point of our conversion (Ephesians 1:13-14). We have personal access to God's presence, power, and Spirit through Christ Jesus. That is incredible, but is not primarily what we are talking about here. David's vision was not mainly about his personal breakthrough or experience. He was longing for something to impact his city and nation. He was longing for corporate breakthrough and revival. He wanted the entire nation to collectively experience what he had already personally experienced in his relationship with God.

The original Hebrew word David used for a "place" for God in Psalm 132:5 is the word māqôm. It typically refers to land or a locality. It can also be translated as "space" or "region." What does it look like for God's glory to rest upon a region? In historic revivals, we have seen glimpses of what can happen when a city or nation comes under the sway of God's manifest presence. It was said of the Welsh revival in the early 1900s that: *"The awe of the Lord was upon everyone and His presence was felt everywhere. Spontaneous prayer meetings began in the mines, factories, schools and shops. Even the amusement parks were filled with a holy awe as brigades of evangelists swept through them. Many who entered taverns to order drinks left them untouched as conviction and the fear of God came upon them."* [5]

That is what David is dreaming about—a dwelling place for God's glory in their land.

A Resting Place

In Psalm 132, David seems to use the terms "dwelling place" and "resting place" interchangeably. However, the phrase "resting place" gives us unique insights into David's vision and God's desire. What does it mean specifically that God would "rest" in a

---

5   Rick Joyner, *The World Aflame: The Welsch Revival and Its Lessons For Our Time.* Charlotte, NC: Morningstar Publications, 1993), 51.

place? The first place we see God rest in the Scriptures is on the seventh day of creation—the Sabbath. What does it mean that God "rested" on the seventh day? It did not mean that God was tired. He does not get weary. God's rest on the sabbath was an indication that the earth had become His resting place. The work was done. It was exactly how He wanted it. There was no tension, no struggle, no fight, no challenge. God had things just as He desired. His will was being done perfectly. Heaven was on earth.[6]

Since sin has come into the world, there is now "unrest" in the world, where the kingdom of darkness is colliding with the kingdom of God. God's will is no longer perfectly done on the earth, although God's desire is to restore His kingdom and perfect will right here, as it is in heaven.

Your kingdom come, your will be done, on earth as it is in heaven (Matthew 6:10).

We could say, then, that God's resting place is a place of God's kingdom. When God can rest in a place, it means that that is a place where everything is submitted to Him. God's resting place is a place where He has complete dominion. It is not just a place of His presence and power, it is a place where He reigns over everything. In God's resting place, an entire group of people and a geographic place come under His divine leadership.

David's desire was not just for a place where Israel could experience God's presence and worship Him, but David was inviting God to come and take His rightful place as King over Israel. David's "resting place" vision was not just for a Temple to be built, but for the very throne room of God to be established in their midst.

---

6   See Beale, *The Temple*, 60-62, for more on the connection between God's sabbath rest and his resting place in the tabernacle.

As we will discover later, even after David established his tent in Zion, he was still not fully satisfied. He longed to build a permanent place for God's presence (I Chronicles 17:1). Yet God would not allow David to do it. It would be his son Solomon who would build the Temple in Jerusalem, and Solomon would read a portion of Psalm 132 at the Temple inauguration (2 Chronicles 6:41-42). The permanent Temple provided a measure of fulfillment of David's vow, but it would be another Son of David who would eventually manifest David's vision for heaven on earth. David's "dwelling place" dream was touching something much broader than God's purposes simply for his generation or his nation. He was connecting to God's heart for the nations of the earth to become resting places of His presence and kingdom.

Zeal for God's House

We know that David was tapping into the heart of God, because Psalm 132:5 indicates that bringing the ark of the covenant into Jerusalem was the desire of the Lord (Psalm 132:5). David's leadership process was to align His life with the will and purposes of God. His life was marked by partnership with God; he wanted what God wanted. Remember Jesus prayed "Father, I desire that they also, whom you have given me, may be with me where I am" (John 17:24). This is the same desire we find in Psalm 132. God longs to be with his people!

> God is looking for presence-pioneers who are willing to seem a little crazy and do whatever it takes to build a dwelling place for His presence—in their hearts, in their homes, and in their cities.

Have you ever felt that raging inferno of God's desire for us? When we touch the very fringe of the zeal of the Lord, we find ourselves overwhelmed and undone. David touched this deep desire in God.

It was a blessing and a curse. David experienced the tension of a prophetic intercessor who saw what God wanted to accomplish, but he was largely misunderstood in his day and time. Solomon witnessed his father's heartaches and so he began Psalm 132 with "Lord, remember David and all his afflictions." David also gave a firsthand account of the reproach that came upon him because of the zeal he had for establishing a place for God. David described some of these hardships in Psalm 69.

> *For it is for your sake that I have borne reproach, that dishonor has covered my face. I have become a stranger to my brothers, an alien to my mother's sons. For **zeal for your house has consumed me**, and the reproaches of those who reproach you have fallen on me. When I wept and humbled my soul with fasting, it became my reproach. When I made sackcloth my clothing, I became a byword to them. I am the talk of those who sit in the gate, and the drunkards make songs about me (Psalm 69:7-12).*

It seems that David's zeal for God's house was the primary source of his affliction. He could not get away from his desire for God's presence. He cried out to God with prayer and fasting, but those acts of desperation became another reason for people to deride him. It says that the drunkards of Israel would sing songs that mocked David because of his zeal for the Lord!

Centuries later, when Jesus cleansed the temple in Jerusalem, his disciples would remember and quote this passage from David. After his first miracle in Cana, we read that Jesus traveled to

Jerusalem for the Passover, and when He saw merchants and money changers in the temple's outer court, He fashioned a whip and drove out those who were there simply to profit from the temple system (John 2:13-21). Jesus was zealous to see the temple as a place for communion with God. In other accounts of the story[7] Jesus quoted Isaiah that His house was to be a "house of prayer," but the religious elite had made it a "den of thieves." Israel had abandoned Davidic worship, and the Jewish leaders had resorted to man-made religious systems disconnected from authentic relationship with God. This is what drove Jesus to his most violent act in the Gospels. He drove out the moneychangers and turned over their tables. His disciples then quote David from Psalm 69 to describe Jesus: "Zeal for your house has consumed me" (John 2:17).

It is only God's zeal in us that can keep us zealous for the long haul.

The same zeal that David had in his heart for a "house" for God's presence was the same zeal Jesus had for a "house of prayer." This was, in fact, the same vision. It was God's dream that He would have a dwelling place on the earth with His people. As we saw in previous chapters, the zeal of Jesus was the zeal of David. Jesus' prayer in John 17:24 reflected David's prayer in Psalm 27:4. And then Jesus's disciples quoted Psalm 69 to describe His fervor. Like David, Jesus's zeal also led to reproach. He would be abandoned by his closest friends, and the crowds that he taught and served would cry out for him to be crucified. Those whom He came to earth to love and save would kill him. His zeal for the house of prayer, to see the kingdom of heaven on the earth, would lead to the greatest affliction in history— namely,

---

7   Perhaps they were separate stories or perhaps they were different accounts of the same story. See Matthew 21:13, Mark 11:17, Luke 19:46.

His death on the cross. While dying, Jesus would quote David again: "My God, My God, why have you forsaken Me?" (Psalm 22:1, Matthew 27:46).

David's Vow

I once asked Nancy, the intercessor I mentioned earlier, how she stayed zealous in prayer and intercession for decades. I was expecting some great prayer tips or strategies. But her response was: "He won't let me go." She had a revelation that it was not her own perseverance that sustained her; it was God's faithfulness towards her that allowed her to stay steady for decades. It is only God's zeal in us that can keep us zealous for the long haul. Likewise, when we connect to the zeal of God and get a vision that is from Him, we will do whatever it takes to see it fulfilled. This is what we find in David's journey.

The unrelenting vision of a "place" for God is what was before David's eyes when he made his vow recorded in Psalm 132. He had connected to God's desire for heaven to come to the earth, and David was ready to make a radical commitment to see the manifestation of the dream in his heart. Here is the vow he made that would set the trajectory of his life:

"Surely I will not go into the chamber of my house or go up to the comfort of my bed; I will not give sleep to my eyes or slumber to my eyelids, until I find a place for the LORD , a dwelling place for the Mighty One of Jacob" (Psalm 132:3).

David overstates his commitment by saying that he would not sleep until the resting place was established. Obviously, it was physically impossible for him to do this. The point is that David was going to allow this vision to interrupt the normal rhythms and conveniences of his life. He was even willing to sacrifice sleep. David's prioritization of God's presence would not be convenient, but it would be worth it. A key word in verse three is "until." David was focused and entirely committed to this vision of God's presence and transformation in Israel. He wasn't sure how long it would take or what the full cost would be, but it did not matter. David was saying that he would do anything he could to see God's presence among His people.

I believe God is inviting us all to be consumed like David— to be gripped with His desire to be with His people. He longs to manifest His presence and kingdom on the earth. He is looking for presence-pioneers who are willing to seem a little crazy and do whatever it takes to build a dwelling place for His presence—in their hearts, in their homes, and in their cities.

On Earth as in Heaven

After establishing the Boiler Room in downtown Greenville, North Carolina, we began to gather the body of Christ to worship and pray for revival in our city and region. We also began to build relationships with other groups in eastern North Carolina who had been pursuing revival for years—even decades. Some of the seasoned intercessors that we met were aware of specific promises from God for our region given in previous years. One of these prophetic words given by Derek Prince provoked us deeply. In 1975, while visiting eastern NC he prophesied:

> *"I have found favor with you here in Eastern North Carolina. I will personally come to visit you. There will be a revival greater than the great Wales phenomenon. There will be kings and leaders from north, south, east, and west that will come and study the Eastern North Carolina phenomenon."*

To be aware of the events during the historic revival in Wales in the early 1900s is to understand how profound a prophetic promise this is for our region. It was reported that 100,000 people came to the Lord in the first year of the revival. Many believe it was the Wales revival that helped sparked the Azusa Street revival in the United States around the same time.[1]

---

1   Frank Bartleman's book *Azusa Street* describes his relationship with Evan Roberts, the unofficial leader of the Wales revival.

As I began to research this prophetic word, I discovered some of the context in which it was given. There was a church in Jacksonville, North Carolina that was being influenced by the Latter Rain revival in the 60s and 70s. One of the resources that had deeply influenced the congregation was *The Power of His Presence* by Graham Truscott. This was the first modern book written on the topic of David's tabernacle. After reading it, the local church began to incorporate Davidic worship into their meetings, and God was moving powerfully. Additionally, they were beginning to experience fellowship and unity with other churches in the area.

In 1975, this group of churches decided to invite Derek Prince in for a series of special meetings. Believers crammed into the sanctuary for the first meeting, which was marked by the presence of God during the music and worship. It was said that "most people cared very little about the apparent lack of space. Only one thing mattered: God was in the house!" Remember, the meetings were taking place in the local church that had begun to incorporate Davidic worship—musical instruments and prophetic songs were beginning to be released. Creativity and intercession were beginning to flow. Another facet of this meeting was the gathering of worshipers from various races and church backgrounds. One attendee said, "We each began to understand that, although our skin pigments and denominations were different, we were indeed one body." [2]

It was in this context that Derek Prince released his prophetic word:

"I have found favor with you here in Eastern North Carolina....."

---

2   Stephen Everett, *The Sound That Changed Everything* (Shippensburg, PA: Treasure House, an imprint of Destiny Image, 2003).

For many years I believed that there was something special about our region. We had found favor with God. Surely we would experience revival before anywhere in the world, right? I thought the prophetic word was about our region, but I was missing the point. One day, as I was praying for God to fulfil this prophetic promise (which I have now done thousands of times), the Holy Spirit broadened my understanding of what He was speaking through Derek Prince.

I realized that the body of Christ was joining in unity around God's presence when this word was released, and it was the context of united, Davidic worship in which God was speaking about His favor! Although God has a unique destiny for every part of the world, this prophetic word was not that our geography was special. It was God's stamp of approval upon His people coming together on earth as in heaven. The church in our region was engaging in Davidic worship in unity with believers of different races and denominations.

This is the environment in which God releases his favor. I realized that this prophetic word speaks not just to our region, but to the body of Christ. If you want God's favor in your region—if you want revival—start doing on earth what is done in heaven. The prophetic promise wasn't just because of a certain geographic location, it was because of a certain activity to which God responds.

Prophetic Insight

Last chapter we began to explore the *why* behind David's tabernacle. One question we have yet to ask is: what inspired the dramatic new expression of worship at David's tabernacle? How did David get the idea to set up day-and-night, prophetic worship music as a means to host the presence of God? There is an important verse that gives us some insight into how David received revelation for establishing his revolutionary order of worship. This insight comes from the story of Hezekiah, when he restored Davidic worship in Israel.

> *And he stationed the Levites in the house of the Lord with cymbals, with stringed instruments, and with harps, according to the commandment of David, of Gad the king's seer, and of Nathan the prophet; for thus was the commandment of the Lord by His prophets (2 Chronicles 29:25).*

This passage makes it clear that the Davidic order of worship was "the commandment of the Lord by His prophets." David's tabernacle was not David's idea, but God's idea. The revelation came through "prophets"—namely Nathan and Gad. Maybe David received direct revelation from the Lord about this too. Perhaps Samuel the prophet was involved in helping David understand this new worship order. We have already described how the schools of prophetic musicians Samuel established seemed to serve as a forerunner to David's tabernacle.

While the Bible does not describe exactly when or how David came to understand God's desire for the new worship order, it is obvious from the verse above that the vision for David's tabernacle was a prophetic revelation given by God, either directly to David or through the prophets that were around him. This eliminates any possibility that David was simply following a whim or passion. He was following the word of the Lord.

A Heavenly Blueprint

I believe that the prophetic revelation David received was insight into the heavenly worship order that is surrounding the throne of God. And I believe this heavenly worship order corresponds to what was established in David's tabernacle.

Understanding the heavenly dimension to Davidic worship will become apparent as we compare the heavenly visions in the Bible to the descriptions of David's worship order.

Other authors have noted this correlation. Jason Hershey connects the importance of the 24/7/365 worship to the incessant worship of the heavenly throne room.[3] John Dickson emphasizes the continuous worship of heaven in his teaching on Davidic worship.[4] Fritch says, "David received a prophetic pattern for replicating the Kingdom of God on earth."[5] I believe understanding this truth is the key to unlocking the revelation God wants to give the church about the importance of David's tabernacle.

The apostle John's visions in Revelation 4 and 5 give us the clearest picture of the heavenly throne room, and the comparisons between the liturgy of the worship scene in heaven to David's tabernacle are stunning.

- The throne is in the center of the heavenly throne room just as the ark was in the center of Jerusalem and David's Tabernacle. Everything centered around God.

- The elders in heaven offer sacrifices of musical praise and intercessory prayer (Revelation 5:8) as ministry to the Lord, just as David's tabernacle introduced "intercessory worship" into the priesthood of Israel.

- In heaven, the four living creatures worship day and night (Revelation 4:8), and David established worship "day and night" in the tent (I Chronicles 9:33).

3   Leithart, *From Silence to Song,* 74-76.

4   John Dickson and Chuck D. Pierce, *Worship As It Is In Heaven* (Ventura, CA: Gospel Light, 2010), 50-51, 101-102.

5   David Fritch, *Enthroned: Bringing God's Kingdom to Earth Through Unceasing Worship & Prayer* (Independently published, 2017), 32.

- Those four living creatures around the throne in heaven compare to the four "fathers" over the worship leaders in the David's tent—David, Asapth, Jeduthun and Heman (I Chronicles 25:1).

- Around the heavenly throne worship is pouring forth from twenty-four elders who lead the host of heaven in musical praise (Rev. 4:10-11, 5:8). King David established twenty-four worship leaders who led the teams of musicians at David's tent (1 Chronicles 25:8-31).

- Around the throne there are thousands upon thousands of angels singing to God night and day (Rev. 5:11). King David also hired four thousand Levites to sing and play instruments to the Lord night and day (1 Chronicles 23:5).

- The antiphony of worship from the various groups described in Revelation 5 reflect the antiphonal worship that was part of the God-ordained Davidic order, as seen clearly in the stories of Nehemiah and Ezra (Ezra 3:11, Nehemiah 12:24).

Incredible! David was not coming up with a new order of worship. He was simply replicating the worship model of heaven on the earth. The worship order of the tabernacle of David is the heavenly worship order! If heaven was David's prophetic inspiration, then David would have wanted to pursue incessant worship in his tabernacle. This realization provides the strongest case for non-stop worship in the tent on Mt Zion. Even if it was not continuous for thirty-three years, I believe David's desire was to do his best to enthrone God in praise perpetually—in Jerusalem as in heaven.

God's Man Cave

As we look more closely at the apostle John's vision of heaven it brings us to another realization: the heavenly *tabernacle* is also the heavenly *throne room*. Perhaps you are familiar with singing worship songs about "entering the throne room" of God; but stop and think about it. The governmental command center of God's kingdom is also a place of Davidic worship. The environment from which the King of Kings releases His grace, His power, and His judgments on the earth is day-and-night songs of praise and intercession!

I like to refer to the heavenly throne room as God's man cave.[6] This is a place where God has things exactly as He wants them. Jesus said in heaven is where God's perfect will is done (Matthew 6:10). And God has voluntarily chosen to have Davidic worship be the atmosphere of heaven. He could have any environment He wants, but He chooses to have the songs and prayers of His people surround Him like incense day and night. This begins to explain the way David brought together the priestly and kingly dimension of Israel during his reign. Although it was unprecedented, David was pursuing a vision of heaven on earth, where there is no separation between the praise and worship of God and the rule and reign of His kingdom.

> **David was not coming up with a new order of worship. He was simply replicating the worship model of heaven on the earth. The worship order of the tabernacle of David is the heavenly worship order!**

---

6   Man cave is a slang term. Wikipedia describes a man cave as a 'sanctuary in a home, such as a specially equipped garage, spare bedroom, media room, den, basement, or tree house. The term "man cave" is a metaphor describing a room where one or more male family members and optionally their friends are supposed to be able to do as they please...' https://en.wikipedia.org/wiki/Man_cave

You Have Come to Mount Zion

Biblically, these themes of worship and government come together in the concept of Zion. The word Zion is used in multiple ways in Scripture, but it always refers to both a place of God's presence and a place of God's rule. The origin of the term Zion was during David's reign in Jerusalem (I Chronicles 11:5).[7] We see throughout the Scriptures that "Zion" or "Mt. Zion" refer specifically to the place of God's people gathered around His presence and offering sacrifices of praise.

Sing praises to the Lord, who sits enthroned in Zion!
(Psalm 9:11).

Praise is due to you, O God, in Zion... (Psalm 65:11).

Zion also refers to a place of God's government, from which He rules, reigns, and releases His judgments.

The Lord will reign forever, your God, O Zion, to all generations
(Psalm 146:10).

"As for me, I have set my King on Zion, my holy hill" (Psalm 2:6).

The Lord sends forth from Zion your mighty scepter. Rule in
the midst of your enemies! (Psalm 110:2).

We have already seen that David may have chosen Jerusalem—Zion—because of Melchizedek, the king-priest who reigned from Jerusalem 600 years before David (Genesis 14:17-20). The place where David's tabernacle was put in place had already been

---

7 The hill on which David's palace and tabernacle were established was the original Mount Zion. However, the term was later applied to the hill on which Solomon's temple was built, even though that hill was actually Mount Moriah (2 Chronicles 3:1). Zion evolved into a poetic term that sometimes described the city of Jerusalem and sometimes described the specific hill upon which God was worshiped.

serving as a "Zion" for centuries. It had already been a place of worship and a place of government in the days of Abraham.

Bringing the concepts together, it becomes obvious that "Zion" is a place of heaven on earth. It is an earthly manifestation of the throne room of God — where the Lord is worshiped day and night and where the Lord reigns over His kingdom. It is both a dwelling place of God's presence and a resting place where God's will is done. With the descriptions of Zion aligning to John's heavenly vision, it is no surprise that the New Testament specifically refers to heaven as "Mount Zion."

But you have come to Mount Zion and to the city of the living God, the heavenly Jerusalem, and to innumerable angels in festal gathering, and to the assembly of the firstborn who are enrolled in heaven, and to God, the judge of all, and to the spirits of the righteous made perfect, and to Jesus, the mediator of a new covenant, and to the sprinkled blood that speaks a better word than the blood of Abel (Hebrews 12:22-24).

Perhaps this verse in Hebrews serves as the most explicit indication that David's tabernacle was a reflection of the heavenly throne room. In this passage heaven is referred to as "Mount Zion" — the very place of David's original worship order. The heavenly Zion is now a spiritual reality. The place of Christian worship is not just in a particular city or in a sacred temple. The place of Christian worship is now in the heavenly place of God's presence that we access through Jesus Christ. The Bible intentionally uses the language of Zion to describe this New Covenant worship. David's kingdom was a picture of the kingdom of God, and Davidic worship is a picture of God's desire for Christian worship —that it would be on earth as it is in heaven.

This heavenly blueprint was the key to the power of David's

tabernacle, and it is why God prophesied through Derek Prince that our region had found God's favor. God likes it when we come together in unity. He likes Davidic worship. That is why it's that way in heaven. That is why there are harps and bowls of incense. That is why there is gathered every tribe, tongue, and nation together (Revelation 5:9, 7:9). If we want historic revival, we need to come together with Christians who are different from us and engage in prophetic, musical, presence-centered praise and worship. That is the heavenly pattern.

"Zion" is a place of heaven on earth. It is an earthly manifestation of the throne room of God — where the Lord is worshiped day and night and where the Lord reigns over His kingdom.

The biblical order attracts God's favor. David discovered it well before his time, and that is why his life, nation, and lineage experienced unprecedented favor and blessing.

A Greater Priesthood

The Lord has sworn and will not change his mind, 'You are a priest forever after the order of Melchizedek" (Psalm 110:4).

We have established that David's tabernacle was modeled after the heavenly throne room, which is both a place of God's presence and a place of God's government. We have also established the fact that "Zion" in Scripture represents the place where heaven and earth come together, which is why it was the original name for the place where David established his tabernacle. One key passage about Zion requires a deeper look.

Psalm 110 is one the most frequently quoted or referenced passages in the New Testament. This very strange Psalm of David seemed to have been extremely important to Jesus (Matt. 22:41-46), Peter (Acts 2:23-24), and the author of Hebrews. It is a bit difficult to understand at first glance, but it is going to help tie together a number of ideas that have been touched on so far. The first two verses of Psalm 110 are a prophetic promise of the coming Messiah who would be the King of God's people, ruling and reigning from Zion. Because the Messiah would reign from "Zion" it's not surprising that verses 3 and 4 show us that this King would also be a Priest. Verse 4 specifically says:

The Lord has sworn and will not change his mind, "You are a
priest forever according to the order of Melchizedek."

Not only would the Messiah be a priest, but he would be "according to the order of Melchizedek." Do you remember Melchizedek? He was the king and priest of God who originally ruled from Jerusalem during the time of Abraham (Genesis 14:17-20). I proposed earlier that the ministry of Melchizedek could have been part of why God desired to have David establish the capital city there. After Abraham's initial encounter with Melchizedek, there is no further mention of this mysterious character until Psalm 110.

Christians believe Jesus is the Messiah prophesied about in Psalm 110. He is the One who will rule the nations from Zion forever. But what does it mean that He is a priest "according to the order of Melchizedek"? In my journey to understand David's tabernacle, the answer to that question was a key that unlocked a door to deeper revelation. Clarity around Jesus's priesthood answered some of my lingering questions about *why* and *how* David established his unprecedented worship order on Mount Zion.

Psalm 110 is one the most frequently quoted or referenced passages in the New Testament.

Thankfully, the book of Hebrews gives us valuable commentary on both Melchizedek and Psalm 110 to help us grasp what David was doing and its implications for us today.

Two Priesthoods

Hebrews describes and contrasts two different priesthoods. The first priesthood was the Levitical priesthood, established through a covenant with Moses on Mount Sinai. This was the priesthood that maintained worship in Moses' portable tabernacle and offered the burnt offerings prescribed in the Law given to Israel. These ongoing sacrifices and rituals kept Israel in good standing with the Lord. Only those who were of the tribe of Levi were part of this priesthood. Admission into this calling was based on an individual's bloodline. Aaron's sons were the specific groups of Levites who served as priests, and only the high priest could go into the inner sanctum of the tabernacle annually to offer a blood sacrifice on the day of atonement. This priesthood system was a temporary solution for the nation of Israel, to provide the means for them to continue in covenant relationship to God until Messiah would come.

Hebrews 7 describes another priesthood that is not like the old Levitical priesthood. Because Jesus Christ has come, a new priesthood has now been established—a new way for all the nations to relate to God. As high priest, Jesus offered his shed blood before the altar in heaven as the final atoning sacrifice for God's people. Entrance into His priesthood is not based on one's physical bloodline, but by coming into the spiritual family of God through Jesus. God has established a new covenant, in contrast to the covenant made with Israel in Sinai, that is entered into by faith in the work of Jesus on the cross. This covenant was sealed by the blood of Jesus and stands forever. Jesus now stands as the eternal intercessor—the only mediator between God and humanity. No one comes to the Father except through Jesus.

We have this as a sure and steadfast anchor of the soul, a hope that enters into the inner place behind the curtain, where Jesus has gone as a forerunner on our behalf, having become a high priest forever after the order of Melchizedek (Hebrews 6:19-20).

For Christ has entered, not into holy places made with hands, which are copies of the true things, but into heaven itself, now to appear in the presence of God on our behalf (Hebrews 8:5).

This new priesthood is a distinctly heavenly priesthood. Jesus ascended to heaven as a forerunner so that His people can follow Him into the very presence of God. Hebrews urges us to "draw near to the throne of grace" with confidence in what Christ has done for us (Hebrews 4:16). We do not come to God through our own merit, but by the merit of Jesus; therefore we have boldness to approach God. Where is this "throne" we approach? The very throne room of God in heaven itself. Spiritually, we can access God's glory and presence *now* because of Jesus. When we draw near to God in prayer, praise, and worship, we "come before the throne of God" in heaven by the blood of the Lamb.

The book of Hebrews goes on to describe our "heavenly calling" (3:1). It says that believers are those who "have tasted the heavenly gift" (Hebrews 6:4). The Levitical priesthood is called a "copy and shadow" of the true heavenly priesthood (Hebrews 8:5). Those who walked by faith in the Old Testament era were those who "desire a better country, that is, a heavenly one" (11:16). And as we've mentioned before, the grand finale of Hebrews is arguably the end of chapter 12, where Mount Sinai—the place where God established the Levitical priesthood with Moses—is contrasted with Mount Zion—which in this case refers to the heavenly city. Remember that Mount Zion also referred to the mountain in Jerusalem where David established his tabernacle.

For you have not come to what may be touched, a blazing fire and darkness and gloom and a tempest and the sound of a trumpet and a voice whose words made the hearers beg that no further messages be spoken to them. For they could not endure the order that was given, "If even a beast touches the mountain, it shall be stoned." Indeed, so terrifying was the sight that Moses said, "I tremble with fear." But you have come to Mount Zion and to the city of the living God, the heavenly Jerusalem... (18-22).

The contrast makes clear that the heavenly priesthood of Zion is superior to the priesthood established on Mount Sinai. Jesus has now made a way for God's people to enter the presence of God by a new and living way (Hebrews 10:19-22).

The Order of Melchizedek

In this heavenly priesthood, Jesus is described as the "high priest according to the order of Melchizedek." The author of Hebrews references Psalm 110 consistently to describe the role of Jesus as both King and Priest, just like Melchizedek. This makes perfect sense because we have already seen that God's heavenly throne room is a place of day-and-night worship and prayer. In heaven, the priestly ministry to the Lord flows together with the kingly rule of God. Whether it is Jerusalem or the heavenly throne room, it is "Mount Zion": the place of priestly worship and the place of God's government. The prophet Zechariah also describes Jesus bringing together the office of priest and king:

"It is he who shall build the temple of the Lord and shall bear royal honor, and shall sit and rule on his throne. And there shall be a priest on his throne, and the counsel of peace shall be between them both" (Zechariah 6:13).

Those of us who are in Christ have become a part of this "royal priesthood" and can now minister to the Lord and be in His presence forever with Jesus! Just as heaven is filled with non-stop praise, the author of Hebrews urges God's people to take advantage of this priesthood by joining in the continuous worship of heaven on the earth.

> *Through him then let us continually offer up a sacrifice of praise to God... (Hebrews 13:15).*

The apostle Peter teaches on these same themes.

> *Coming to Him... you also, as living stones, are being built up a spiritual house, a holy priesthood, to offer up spiritual sacrifices acceptable to God through Jesus Christ... But you are a chosen generation, a royal priesthood, a holy nation, His own special people, that you may proclaim the praises of Him who called you out of darkness into His marvelous light (1 Peter 2:4-5,9).*

The church is called a priesthood, and this means that we are priests. As priests the Bible instructs us to offer up "spiritual sacrifices" to God through Jesus. It describes the body of Christ as "living stones" who are being built together by God as a spiritual tabernacle. Why? So we can "proclaim the praises" of Jesus. This echoes the call in Hebrews to offer God a "sacrifice of praise." In Jesus, our worship becomes our priestly ministry. Our praise becomes our offerings.

The sacrifices we offer God in this royal priesthood are not atoning sacrifices. To be clear, our worship is not earning anything from the Lord. All our spiritual sacrifices are offered to God in light of the ultimate sacrifice Christ has made for us. He paid the price. He earned our access to God's righteousness, salvation, and love. We are simply responding to what He has already done as we lay down our lives as living sacrifices and pour out our praises to him.

> *Therefore, I urge you, brothers and sisters, in view of God's mercy, to offer your bodies as a living sacrifice, holy and pleasing to God—this is your true and proper worship (Romans 12:1).*

Paul also uses the priestly language of sacrifice to describe our proper response to the gospel. Jesus made a way for us to become who were designed to be: priests and kings to God forever. The most honoring thing we can do in light of the cross of Christ is to take advantage of what He has done and enter fully into our calling to worship the Lord and host His presence in our lives, churches, and cities.

The Priesthood of David's Tabernacle

This heavenly priesthood we are describing is the reality in which David's tabernacle was functioning. We have already established that the worship in David's tabernacle was modeled after the heavenly throne room. Now we have also seen that the heavenly throne room operates in a royal priesthood according to the order of Melchizedek, which is distinct from the Levitical priesthood.

I believe David's tabernacle was not only following the heavenly *worship model*, but it was functioning within the heavenly *priesthood*. This explains why there were two tabernacles during David's reign in Jerusalem. The tabernacle at Gibeon was functioning under the Levitical priesthood of Moses, but the tabernacle in Jerusalem was functioning under the heavenly priesthood. God had given prophetic revelation to David, even before Jesus had come to the earth, of His eternal priesthood. David's tabernacle was functioning in that which was eternal and prophesying of that which was to come in Christ. Theologian Scott W. Hahn says, "If David was indeed a new Melchizedek, Christ is the definitive new Melchizedek."[1] He goes on to lay out the unmistakable theological connections between David's tabernacle and the priesthood of Melchizedek.[2]

---

1   Scott Hahn, *The Kingdom of God as Liturgical Empire* (Grand Rapids, MI: Baker Academic, 2012), 66.

2   Hahn, *Kingdom of God,* 58-61.

The fact that David's tabernacle functioned in an entirely different priesthood begins to explain the ways in which David was seemingly breaking the law and getting away with it.

For when there is a change in the priesthood, there is neces-sarily a change in the law as well (Hebrews 7:12).

Once the tent was established in Zion, the worshipers were not functioning under the protocol of the Levitical priesthood at all! So, no laws were being broken. The animal sacrifices had ended in Zion and the sacrifices of praises had begun. It was a new order, a new system, and a new priesthood. All the Levitical procedures were relegated to the other tabernacle in Gibeon.

> **David's tabernacle was functioning in that which was eternal and prophesying of that which was to come in Christ.**

Some have tried to attribute the revolutionary approach of David's tabernacle to David's unique intimacy with the Lord, as if somehow God would allow David to "break the rules" because of their close relationship. I find this untenable. David's intimacy with the Lord would have given him a deep desire to obey God and His Word, not defy it. It was David who wrote the great love song to God's law in Psalm 119. David wasn't breaking the Law; he was following a higher law.

Think about it like this. An airplane continues to fly despite the law of gravity. Yet it flies not because it has annulled the law of gravity, but because it has taken advantage of a greater law—the law of lift. David was not annulling the law of Moses, but he brought Israel into an entirely different priesthood with a different set of rules during those thirty-three years.

I believe this helps explain David's dramatic departure from

Israel's norms that some have called the "Davidic Liturgical Revolution."[3] Before David's reign, the only music at the Mosaic tabernacle came from the trumpets used to gather Israel for assembly. Even those trumpets were not sounded as an expression of praise to the Lord. The burnt offerings were the sacrifices offered to God, not the sacrifices of praise. David introduced a revolutionary new order of worship—namely, day and night, prophetic, intercessory worship that reflected the throne room of heaven. In David's tabernacle, the songs became the sacrifices. Why this shift? Because it is the worship order of the heavenly priesthood.

This explains why David and the Levites had unprecedented access to God's presence, without the limitation of the veil that separated God's people in the Mosaic tabernacle. During the ark procession David wore a linen ephod, a priestly garment, and in 1 Chronicles 17:16 it says David "went in and sat before the Lord" and simply started talking to Yahweh in the tent. David himself was able to function as a priest before God, even though he was from the tribe of Judah. While the Levitical priesthood required a person to be of the tribe of Levi to minister before the Lord, the heavenly priesthood allows anyone to enter into God's presence by faith in the Messiah. David was a priest, to be sure, but of a different priesthood altogether.

This explains why the Gentiles were also invited into the tabernacle of David. You may remember that Obed-Edom was the Gentile who housed the ark of the covenant between David's two attempts to bring it into Jerusalem. His household experienced great blessing while the ark rested there (2 Samuel 6:11). Curiously, you find an "Obed Edom" serving as a gatekeeper in David's tabernacle. It's likely that he was so touched

---

3   Leithart, *From Silence to Song.*

by God's presence that he followed the ark to Israel and became incorporated into the tabernacle of David.[4] Additionally, the very first song that was sung at David's tabernacle was not just about Israel but about all the nations of the earth worshiping Yahweh (I Chronicles 16:23-24). The Levitical priesthood was limited to the old covenant made with ethnic Israel, so this inaugural song only makes sense when you realize that the heavenly priesthood is for all the nations. That is why Obed-Edom could serve as a gatekeeper and why the first song in David's tabernacle included an invitation for all people to come worship the Lord—because the heavenly throne room includes every "tribe and language and people and nation" gathered in unity as kings and priests to God (Rev. 5:9-10). I believe the inclusion of Gentiles at David's tabernacle was only possibly because David had established the heavenly priesthood on the earth.

We can follow the thread from the original Melchizedek in Jerusalem, who served as a king and priest, to King David, who established his tabernacle in the same place and served as both a priest and the king. David called this place Zion—the place where the priestly and kingly ministries come together. It was David who prophesied of the coming Messiah who would rule from Zion and be a priest according to the order of Melchizedek. David's entire tabernacle was modeled after the heavenly worship pattern we see in Revelation 4-5. In the New Testament, the "royal priesthood" is the church. Heaven is described as "Mount Zion," and Jesus the Messiah is described as the high priest of the eternal priesthood. From Melchizedek to David to Jesus, we see God's original desire for a kingdom of priests who would enjoy His presence, minister to Him, and steward the earth as a resting place for God and His Kingdom.

---

4   Leithart, *From Silence to Song*, 43-46.

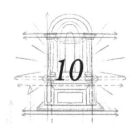

We Were Made for This

"Worthy are you to take the scroll and to open its seals, for you were slain, and by your blood you ransomed people for God from every tribe and language and people and nation, and you have made them a kingdom and priests to our God, and they shall reign on the earth" (Revelation 5:9-10).

When we launched our Boiler Room in Greenville in 2009, I was not exactly sure what to do with the building God had given us. Typically, a ministry moves into a building because they have outgrown a previous space; the facility grows based on the ministry. However, we started with an empty building. We had been hosting some sporadic worship and prayer events, but God had told us that He now wanted His glory to "dwell" in that building. We knew that 24/7 worship and prayer might never be feasible with our small community, but we thought, if God is enthroned on praises, we should offer as much worship and prayer in that room as we possibly could.

When we finally got the prayer room set up and the Boiler Room launched, we moved our Friday night meetings there. But what would we do the other six days of the week? I was a full-time prayer missionary, but our ministry had no other staff. My wife Shepard and I decided to go to the prayer room every weekday morning for a few hours and just worship. I opened it up to others to join us, but many times no one else showed up. At most, there might be a few people in the room at any given moment. On top of everything else, our first child was born a few months after the prayer room opened. During those early days, I recall my wife sitting on a couch in the back of the prayer room, nursing our newborn baby while I sat up front with my guitar singing love songs to Jesus every morning. At one of those first prayer meetings, no more than two or three people came in all morning. But one of them dropped $100 in the donation box. It was a small token, but at the time it was a great encouragement to me that God saw what we were doing as valuable.

These early prayer room days were so vital in helping us learn to *minister to God*. So many activities and events are man-centered, but worship and prayer are supposed to be God-centered. I had grown up leading worship in youth groups, Sunday services, and campus ministries. But now I was in an empty room learning how to pour my heart out to God, whether there were two people in the room on Monday morning or 100 people in the room on a Friday night. In this season, I was learning to be a priest before God. I was learning the value of ministry to the Lord with my songs and prayers. I would think back to my summer camp encounter and the girl Katie who couldn't sing. God let me hear the song of her heart, and it reassured me that my weak worship was a beautiful offering to Him. I realized God was receiving my praise as "incense" to Him—a pleasing aroma that touched His heart. Song of Solomon 4:9 says that the bride "ravishes" the heart of the Bridegroom with one glance from her eyes. The Bible says we are the bride of Christ, which means that Jesus the Bridegroom can be moved by our worship! God doesn't need anything and He never changes, but something about our pursuit of Him captivates His heart.

After some of the initial awkwardness of singing to an empty room wore off, I began to discover the liberty and joy of simply ministering to the Lord. I began to sense His smile towards me as I approached Him. I began to be set free of people-pleasing and performance. My worship began to flow purely from my heart to His. It felt like I was uncovering my destiny. Somehow, standing before God, even in a relatively empty room, seemed like what I was made to do.

> I realized God was receiving my praise as "incense" to Him—a pleasing aroma that touched His heart.

Israel As a Kingdom of Priests

Likewise, when King David set up the tent and established a royal priesthood on Mount Zion, he was tapping into God's original intention for Israel. He was touching God's eternal desire for all His people to minister to Him. The establishment of the limited Levitical priesthood was actually not God's first plan for the nation of Israel. If you know the Exodus story, then you know that God delivered the twelve tribes from bondage in Egypt, and His vision for Israel from the beginning of their journey was that their entire nation would be a "kingdom of priests" that worship the Lord and host His presence.

You yourselves have seen what I did to the Egyptians, and how I bore you on eagles' wings and brought you to myself. Now therefore, if you will indeed obey my voice and keep my covenant, you shall be my treasured possession among all peoples, for all the earth is mine; and you shall be to me a kingdom of priests and a holy nation (Exodus 19:4-6).

It should be obvious that Peter draws from this language in 1 Peter 2:9 when he describes the Church as "a chosen race, a royal priesthood, a holy nation, a people for his own possession." This privileged place of the priesthood is now every believer's honor and duty. And it was God's original intent for the entire nation of Israel to enter collectively into a priesthood as well. Yet when Moses ascended Mount Sinai to receive commandments from God, the nation chose to build and worship an idolatrous golden calf in place of Yahweh. When Moses came down the mountain and rebuked Israel, it was the tribe of Levi that stood faithful to the Lord (Exodus 32:26–29). So God established the Levites, and more specifically the sons of Aaron, to serve as the priesthood within Israel, rather than the entire nation.

When David became king and established the new order of worship, he was, in some ways, helping bring Israel back into that original purpose of being a royal priesthood. Although the Levites were still prominent in their role at the tent, we see David and Obed-Edom also serving in priestly roles, even though they were not of the tribe of Levi. In fact, Obed-Edom was a Gentile. Again, David tapped into something eternal that was in God's heart for all the nations of the earth.

A Royal Priesthood

Just as David was given unprecedented access to God's presence, even though he did not deserve it, God has given us unearned access to His presence through the blood of Jesus, our High Priest. Now we minister to the Lord as priests as we lay down our lives as living sacrifices, and giving God our praise and worship as an offering to Him. This priestly ministry will not end when Christ returns. We will worship forever. Spiritual gifts will cease (1 Cor. 13:8). Evangelism and missions will be unnecessary. But our worship, praise, and intercession will continue into eternity.

According to the book of Revelation, our eternal occupation will be as kings and priests, ministering to the Lord and reigning with Him on the earth.

To him who loves us and has freed us from our sins by his blood and made us <u>a kingdom, priests</u> to his God and Father, to him be glory and dominion forever and ever. Amen (Revelation 1:5-6).

"Worthy are you to take the scroll and to open its seals, for you were slain, and by your blood you ransomed people for God from every tribe and language and people and nation, and you have made them <u>a kingdom and priests</u> to our God, and they shall reign on the earth" (Revelation 5:9-10).

It is clear in these verses that one of the primary purposes of the death and resurrection of Jesus was to establish His people as a "kingdom of priests" to God. This is why Jesus has "freed us from our sins by his blood." The heavenly hosts praise Jesus that He has "ransomed people for God from every tribe and language

> **David tapped into something eternal that was in God's heart for all the nations of the earth.**

and people and nation" by His blood. Unto what end? So we could be priests and kings. Ministering to the Lord is our destiny. If we do not understand what it means to be a "royal priesthood" then we haven't yet begun to grasp God's eternal purpose for our existence. We will be worshiping the Lord and stewarding the earth with Him forever.

The Function of Priests and Kings

What does it mean to be a royal priesthood? How do we do it? While being sons and daughters is our primary identity in the kingdom of God, being priests and kings is our primary function in the kingdom of God. If Jesus is a priest and king forever, then we as His bride will partner with Him in that calling. As Christians, what exactly does it mean practically for us to be priests or kings?

While being sons and daughters is our primary identity in the kingdom of God, being priests and kings is our primary function in the kingdom of God.

As priests we primarily minister to God by worshiping, praying, and serving Him with all of our hearts and lives. We enjoy Him, fellowship with Him, and interact with Him in loving, intimate relationship while offering Him spiritual sacrifices of praise, and partnering with Him in intercession. This "vertical" ministry to God is to be the primary joy and responsibility of every believer. This is what sons and daughters of God do because God's house (a.k.a. family) is a house of prayer (Is 56:7). Ministers and pastors are not the "priests" of Christianity—every believer is a priest unto God through Jesus Christ.

As kings we steward the earth with God, working with Him to manifest His kingdom on earth and bring everything under His dominion, so that God has a resting place where His will is always done (Matthew 6:10). To be clear, God is the supreme "King of Kings" and our kingliness does not make us gods. We have no authority or power in ourselves. As King of the earth, God gives His authority to us to steward His will on the earth. Under the canopy of this "kingly" ministry are things like evangelism, missions, our marketplace work, praying for the sick, caring for the poor, and all the "horizontal" ministries described in the New Testament.

These are not two separate roles, but two intertwined realities that flow from a place of intimacy with God. Our priesthood must be royal, and our kingship must be priestly. You cannot have one without the other. We must love God *and* love others (Matt 22:37-39). We must wait on the Lord (Luke 24:49) *and* go into all the world and make disciples (Matt. 28:19-20). We obey the Great Commandment and the Great Commission. The church must embrace the fullness of our calling as a royal priesthood, functioning as priests who minister to the Lord in worship and prayer, and functioning as kings who minister to others to see salvation, healing, and transformation. This is what we were made to do.

Back to the Beginning

When sharing the story of David's tabernacle, the author of I Chronicles begins with lists of genealogies. He starts at the very beginning, with Adam. He does not begin with Abraham, Isaac, or Jacob. He is making his intention clear. This story he is about to tell about David's tabernacle is reframing the entire story of mankind. Something in David's story connects all the way back to the beginning of time.

Leithart says the author's use of Adam is "an initial clue that the history of the monarchy recapitulates the history of humanity and of Israel between Adam and David."[1] In light of David's emphasis on worship and music, Leithart also states that this reference to Adam implies that "God created Adam to produce a race of singers. Israel exhibits the destiny of humanity: to be brought into God's choir to sing in God's heavenly city."[2]

---

1   Peter Leithart, *1 & 2 Chronicles* (Grand Rapids, MI: Brazos Press, 2019), 14.

2   Leithart, *From Silence to Song,* 13.

In other words, we were created to worship. Being a royal priesthood is not only our *eternal* purpose, but it is our *original* purpose. At the center of our design is the desire and capacity to delight in, respond to, praise, and enjoy God. David's tabernacle created an environment in which God's people could be who they were made to be and do what they were made to do. That is the reason understanding David's tabernacle is not just for worship leaders, singers, musicians, pastors, or missionaries. It is for anyone who wants to find meaning and purpose in life. David's worship order and kingdom connect to something at the heart of every man and woman because we were created for God's presence.

Eden: A Tabernacle of God's Presence

This original design in God's creation becomes even more explicit as we look back at the story of Adam and Eve in the garden of Eden. A closer look will transform our ideas of what occurred in the early days of God's creation. We know that when God created Adam, He placed him in a garden in Eden and gave him responsibility to care for it.

The Lord God took the man and put him in the garden of Eden to work it and keep it (Genesis 2:15).

Depending on your experience, your mental image of this scenario may vary. I personally grew up in rural eastern North Carolina. My dad grew tomatoes and cucumbers in our backyard. My grandfather and uncle owned acres of land where they grew crops like corn and beans. This is what I envision when I hear "garden"—vegetables. Perhaps when you hear the word "garden" you envision a beautiful flower garden, or even a vineyard.

However, the ancient Hebrews would have interpreted this verse in Genesis 2:15 quite differently than any of us. Most scholars believe that it was Moses who wrote the book of Genesis. So this book was written in the context of Moses's life where, in his day, the Israelites were traveling through the wilderness with the tabernacle. They would gather their tribes around this portable tent that housed the ark of the covenant, and the tribe of Levi would be responsible for taking care of it day and night.

God says in Genesis 2:15 that Adam was in the garden to "work" and "keep" it. It is not obvious in English, but there is something unique about the original Hebrew words that are translated "work" and "keep." When the Hebrew people would hear these words together they would not envision vegetables; they would envision a tabernacle. This combination of words were the terms used to describe the Levites who cared for the tabernacle in the wilderness. The Holy Spirit inspired these words to also describe Adam as he took care of the garden of Eden. When Israel heard Adam's job description in Genesis 2:15 they would have immediately thought about the Levites. They would have recognized Eden as a sanctuary and Adam as a priest.[3]

This is an entirely different way of viewing Eden! Adam was not just created to take care of plants. He was created as a priest and a king. Eden was to be a temple of God and Adam was its caretaker. He was to "serve" God—to worship and minister to the Lord as a priest. And he was to "keep" the garden—to steward Eden as God's resting place as a king. He was a guardian of the place of God's presence, just as the Levites were in David's tabernacle.

---

3   Beale, *The Temple and the Church's Mission,* 66. He says, "Gen 2:15 says God placed Adam in the Garden 'to cultivate it and to keep it.' The two Hebrew words for 'cultivate and keep' (respectively, oabad and shamar) can easily be, and usually are, translated 'serve and guard.' When these two words occur together later in the OT, without exception they have this meaning and refer either to Israelites 'serving and guarding/obeying' God's word (about 10 times) or, more often to priests who 'serve' God in the temple and 'guard' the temple from unclean things entering it (Num 3:7–8; 8:25–26; 18:5–6; 1 Chr 23:32; Ezek 44:14)."

This concept of Eden as a tabernacle is confirmed in a vision from the prophet Ezekiel.

You were in Eden, the garden of God... On the day that you were created.... You were the anointed cherub who covers, And I placed you there. You were on the holy mountain of God; You walked in the midst of the stones of fire (Ezekiel 28:13-14).

Eden was a place of worship. The one spoken about in this passage is like a "cherub." You may recall that the ark of the covenant was fashioned with images of golden cherubim on top. These cherubim were the heavenly hosts that were associated with the convergence points of heaven and earth. Those in the garden were like these cherubim because in the days of Eden, heaven and earth were together. God himself was on the earth.

Ezekiel also describes the holy mountain of God in Eden— which is synonymous with a place of God's presence in Scripture. Both Eden and Zion served as mountaintop dwelling places of God's presence. This holy mountain in the garden explains how Eden has multiple rivers flowing from it (Genesis 2:10). Ezekiel also saw a river flowing from under the throne in God's temple (Ezekiel 47:1), and the apostle John saw the same vision—a river flowing from the heavenly throne of God (Revelation 22:1). Clearly, the biblical imagery of Eden is of a heavenly mountain with the throne of God serving as a Temple of the Lord. Interestingly, the rivers are described (Gen 2:10-14) right before Adam is described with his priestly assignment (Gen. 2:15). Between the mountain imagery and the language used to describe Adam's role, it would have been obvious to the Hebrew people what Moses was implying: Adam was a priest and Eden was a tabernacle.

The description of Eden in Ezekiel 28 includes a reference

to a particular being who was there in Eden with God. Some teachers believe it refers to Satan, but others believe that it points to Adam. I am more inclined to believe that it describes Adam there in the garden with God. I do not believe God created Satan/Lucifer as the first "worship leader" as some assert. I believe He created Adam as the first worship leader, especially in light of our new understanding of Genesis 2:15. Adam was clearly described in Genesis as a priest to God who was called to worship the Lord and steward the garden.

If you know the Genesis story, you know that Adam failed in his assignment. Rather than maintaining a pure place of worship, he allowed Satan to come into the garden and bring accusations against God. Adam and Eve believed the lies of the enemy, fell into sin, and were cast out of the garden. It would take the death and resurrection of Jesus to begin the restoration of humanity back to Eden.

> God's original vision of a global tabernacle will be fulfilled in Christ, and the earth will be filled with the knowledge of the glory of the Lord

This understanding of Adam as a royal priest in the garden of Eden gives us a brand-new perspective about God's original purpose for mankind. The earth was created as a dwelling place for God, and humanity was created as the royal priesthood of this global temple. Our original purpose and eternal destiny is to minister to the Lord, be in His presence, worship Him, and tend the earth as a tabernacle of God's glory!

God's command to Adam to "be fruitful and multiply" (Genesis 1:28) now takes on a whole new meaning. God was inviting Adam and Eve to multiply Eden across the planet. He was literally urging them to have babies and fill the earth with worshiping people. This was God's dream for the world. The earth would be full of God's glory as every tribe, tongue, and nation loved Him in unity—hosting God's presence and partnering with Him to care for the earth. Earth was created to be a sanctuary for God. We were made to be a kingdom of priests with God forever. This is why we exist.

And this is why 1 Chronicles begins with "Adam." David was like a new Adam. A new worship leader. A new priest. Hahn says, "Perhaps in David we are meant to see expressed the 'priestly soul' intended for all humanity in the beginning."[4] David's tabernacle was like a new Eden. But it was not the full restoration that was needed. It was a limited snapshot—a prophetic picture of what was to come. It was not the fullness of God's vision. David's tabernacle pointed to the ultimate reality that Jesus Christ is the true second Adam (Romans 5:12-21). He did not fail or fall like the first Adam. He is a faithful High Priest and King. His death and resurrection began the restoration process of all things. Though sin had corrupted the world, He is bringing all things in heaven and earth together again (Ephesians 1:10). God's original vision of a global tabernacle will be fulfilled in Christ, and the earth will be filled with the knowledge of the glory of the Lord (Habakkuk 2:14). God will have a royal priesthood. David's tabernacle was a short-term, localized expression of that priesthood, but the Son of David is now manifesting that restoration globally. God's original vision for Eden will come to pass.

---

4   Hahn, *The Kingdom of God*, 61.

The Promised Restoration

"On that day I will raise up the tabernacle of David, which has fallen down, and repair its damages; I will raise up its ruins, And rebuild it as in the days of old" (Amos 9:11).

From Genesis to Revelation, God has revealed His desire for His people to function as a kingdom of priests. Sin had separated us from God and taken us away from this original purpose, but Jesus is restoring us back to God to be who we were made to be. We were uniquely crafted to worship the Lord and steward the earth as a tabernacle of His presence and kingdom.

David uniquely tapped into this eternal purpose of God when he established his tabernacle and kingdom in Israel. No one else in the Old Testament, aside from Melchizedek, acted as both king and priest. David is one of the most blatant Old Testament types of Jesus Christ, and his kingdom is one of the clearest Old Testament types of the kingdom of heaven. This is part of why understanding David's tabernacle is so important.

In Amos 9:11, God promises to rebuild the tabernacle of David. Nowhere in Scripture does God promise to rebuild Moses's tabernacle or Solomon's temple, yet He promises to rebuild David's tabernacle. What David did is particularly relevant for us as New Testament Christians. The apostle James even quotes this prophecy during the Jerusalem Council in Acts 15:16-17, which we will examine more closely later.

What exactly is this prophesied restoration or rebuilding of David's tabernacle?

A Seed of Revelation

In the early 1960s, at a pastor's conference in New Zealand, the Holy Spirit dropped a seed of revelation about David's Tabernacle that grew in influence throughout a generation and still bears fruit today. The pastors who gathered there had all been touched by what was called the "Latter Rain" revival that broke out in 1948 in Canada. A prophet named David Schoch was teaching at one of the sessions, and the Lord spontaneously shifted the direction of his teaching. He began to prophesy that God was not interested in restoring Moses's tabernacle, but David's tabernacle. I was provided a copy of a personal interview with David Schoch from 2001 where he recalls the incident like this:

> *The understanding of the Tabernacle of David was not part of my message but the Lord shifted gears in my mind and I found myself speaking for the Lord. I heard the words coming from my mouth and I was surprised! I had been thinking about Moses' Tabernacle and Solomon's Temple earlier that afternoon and I heard myself saying that God wasn't interested in doing anything with Solomon's Temple but He was going to restore David's Tabernacle and I turned to Acts 15 and began to speak about this more fully as the Lord revealed it "on the spot."*

God had already laid the groundwork within the Latter Rain movement to receive this word about Davidic worship. As I mentioned previously, Reg Layzell had begun to teach about the importance of worship and how God is enthroned on praises. Spontaneous praise and singing in tongues had already spread throughout the movement in the 1950s. But now God was providing a deeper biblical foundation upon which to build their theology about praise and worship.

David uniquely tapped into the eternal purpose of God when he established his tabernacle and kingdom in Israel. No one else in the Old Testament, aside from Melchizedek, acted as both king and priest.

As best as I can tell, this prophetic word that was dropped at the 1960s pastor's conference in New Zealand was the birthplace of modern teaching on David's tabernacle. According to Schoch, the missionary Graham Truscott listened to a tape from that meeting, heard the prophetic word, and began a personal Bible study on King David. By 1969, Truscott released the first book on the topic called *The Power of God's Presence*.

Kevin Conner describes the developments like this:

"... he had dropped a Divine Seed-Word. Several of the brethren in New Zealand picked it up and God watered this Seed-Word and thus the Scriptures opened up in a whole neglected area concerning worship and the Tabernacle of David." [1]

Conner himself was one who began a personal deep dive into what the Bible says about Davidic worship. His workbook, simply titled *The Tabernacle of David,* was released in the 70s and became one of the major avenues God used to disseminate the David's tabernacle message to the broader body of Christ. Schoch released his prophetic word like a seed into a generation, but even

---

1   Kevin Conner, *This is My Story* (Self-published, 2007), 199-200.

he believed there was still much to learn about David's tabernacle. He said in 2001:

I don't believe we're through with all that God wants to speak about David's Tabernacle, yet. We've only touched a part of it.

After nearly four decades of teachings, study, books, and practice around the theme of Davidic worship, the prophet says "We've only touched part of it."

Conflicting Views About Restoration

Various interpretations of Amos 9:11 and Acts 15:16-17 are debated among Bible teachers and theologians today. In my journey, as I began to discover the story of David's tabernacle, it was primarily from voices in the charismatic branch of Christianity who would tout Amos 9:11 as a reference to the restoration of Davidic *worship*. They would point to the global expansion of day-and-night worship and prayer and see it as part of the fulfillment of the "restoration of the tabernacle of David" that had been prophesied. Their perception was that prophetic singing, day-and-night prayer, creative music, dancing, and the presence of God were at the core of God's promises in Amos 9 and Acts 15. I was exhilarated to discover these ideas, because God had already spoken clearly to me about the importance of David's story in my own life.

As I began to study these passages more deeply, though, I became troubled. Nearly every Bible commentary I looked at had an entirely different understanding of them. Most Bible scholars taught that the "tabernacle" of David was a metaphor for David's dynasty—His royal line. They would explain that Jesus now sits on the "throne of David" (see Acts 2:32-36) and therefore the tabernacle of David had already been restored. In their view, there was no present-day fulfilment of these prophecies—it was already done when Christ ascended to heaven. This was puzzling and disheartening. Why were these well-studied teachers seeing David's restored tabernacle as the *kingdom* of David, rather than the *worship* of David? I was confused. Meanwhile, it seemed that many of the charismatic leaders who were promoting Davidic worship were simply quoting one another, without having any deep biblical roots to support their claims.

I wrestled in prayer and study around these two different interpretations of Amos 9:11. David Fritch labels these two perspectives as the "Charismatic View" and the "Evangelical View" of this restoration.[2] The charismatic teaching is that the rebuilding of David's tabernacle is happening right now as the Church embraces day and night, prophetic worship and prayer. The evangelical teaching says that the restoration of David's tabernacle is a reference to Jesus's reign over the kingdom of God; that David's "tabernacle" is simply a metaphor for the house or lineage of David.

However, with the groundwork I have already laid in previous chapters, we can see how both of these interpretations have merit and are not mutually exclusive. One view is focused on the *priestly* elements of David's leadership and one view is focused on the *kingly* elements of David's reign. David's kingdom and tabernacle were flowing and functioning together to manifest heaven in Israel, and biblically we cannot separate the ideas of worship and government. Zion, the heavenly throne room, is both a place of God's rule *and* a place of day and night worship. There is actually no contradiction in the two interpretations. It's not an either/or issue. David's tabernacle was about both worship *and* the kingdom. In fact, that is a big part of what made it so unique and powerful. It should be no surprise that the restoration of

---

2   Fritch, *Enthroned,* 12-13.

David's "tabernacle" will also contain both a priestly and a royal dimension.

A Throne in The Tent

What the "charismatic view" of Amos 9:11 sometimes fails to take into account is that David's tabernacle was not just about an order of worship but about the establishment of God's will and kingdom on the earth. David was not just establishing a new expression of the priesthood; he was invoking the heavenly worship pattern to invite God to manifest His kingdom in Israel. He was bringing together the priesthood and the kingdom to foreshadow Jesus, who is the King of the universe and the High Priest of the eternal, heavenly priesthood. David's tabernacle is as much about the kingdom as it is about worship. Any honest Bible student will have to acknowledge that Amos 9:11 and Acts 15:16-17 do not talk explicitly about worship at all. Something bigger is going on here.

What the "evangelical view" fails to consider is the atmosphere in which both David and Jesus rule and reign—namely, the atmosphere of day-and-night musical worship and intercession. This view fails to acknowledge the necessity of the priesthood in the kingdom of God. The Davidic order of worship was not just a peculiar oddity of David's reign; it was at the core of his leadership strategy. Centering the nation around God's presence with day-and-night worship was the environment in which God was able to manifest justice, victory, and unity for His people. Without the priesthood of David there was no kingdom of David. This is reinforced by Isaiah's messianic prophecy that includes a reference to David's tabernacle.

"Then a throne will be established in steadfast love, and on it will sit in faithfulness in the tent of David one who judges and seeks justice and is swift to do righteousness" (Isaiah 16:5).

Isaiah prophesies that because of God's steadfast love, Jesus will be established on his throne forever. Where is this throne? In the tent of David; in David's tabernacle. God rules in the midst of worship. He is enthroned in the praises of His people forever. Isaiah 16:5 is clear: the throne upon which Jesus sits is *in* the tabernacle of David. The tabernacle and the throne are not the same thing. R.A Martinez says "There is a throne in the tabernacle. There was one in David's day. There is one in our day. And there will be one forever in the age to come."[3]

The promised restoration of David's tabernacle speaks to both the reign of the Son of David as King and to the restoration of God's people as a royal priesthood in His kingdom. The prophesied "tabernacle" of Amos 9:11 includes both the rule of Jesus on the throne of David *and* the Davidic worship of the church. "Amos' prophecy of a restored Davidic booth is both a promise fulfilled in Jesus, and a promise fulfilled in Jesus' disciples."[4]

We are beginning to see that the simple idea from David that God is enthroned on praises (Psalm 22:3) carries far more weight than it initially seemed. Our worship does not just allow us to experience God's presence, but it is fully part of God's ultimate plan to bring His kingdom to the earth through Jesus Christ.

Revivals of Davidic Worship In Israel's History

There is another factor that implies that Amos was referring to more than just the Davidic kingdom. Throughout the history of Israel, following David's reign, the kings of Israel would vacillate between revival and apostasy. As you study the kings who pursued the Lord and led Israel into seasons of revival, you

---

3   https://www.mapsglobal.org/blog/the-worship-order-of-david
4   Leithart, *From Silence to Song*, 95.

will notice a stunning trend: they adopted Davidic worship. When the nation would turn back to God, the people would also turn back to worshiping the Lord the way David did. Hezekiah, Josiah, Joash, Nehemiah, and Ezra all reinstituted the Davidic worship order during their reigns as king. In each spiritual awakening, the Levites would take their priestly place to minister before God again with day-and-night songs of praise. We'll briefly look at those revivals now.

The promised restoration of David's tabernacle speaks to both the reign of the Son of David as King and to the restoration of God's people as a royal priesthood in His kingdom.

First of all, David's son Solomon continued the Davidic worship order in the permanent temple in Jerusalem.

> *The priests stood at their posts; the Levites also, with the instruments for music to the Lord that King David had made for giving thanks to the Lord—for his steadfast love endures forever—whenever David offered praises by their ministry; opposite them the priests sounded trumpets, and all Israel stood (2 Chronicles 7:6).*

I also must mention King Jehoshaphat, who began ruling around 870 BC. While his story does not reference David specifically, it's worth noting how he employed singers to go before the army and release songs of praise. As they sang, Scripture says that God supernaturally "set an ambush" for the enemies of His people (2 Chronicles 20:21-22). Clearly, Jehoshaphat understood the power of Davidic worship.

The rest of the revivals in Israel's history make explicit

reference to David when they reestablish worship to the Lord. In approximately 715 BC Hezekiah cleansed and consecrated the temple, and then reinstituted the Davidic order of worship (2 Chronicles 29-30).

And he stationed the Levites in the house of the Lord with cymbals, harps, and lyres, <u>according to the commandment of David</u> and of God the king's seer and of Nathan the prophet, for the commandment was from the Lord through his prophets (2 Chronicles 29:25).

Around 705 BC the priest Jehoida, under the direction of King Joash, revived the Davidic worship order (2 Chronicles 23:1–24:27).

And Jehoiada posted watchmen for the house of the Lord under the direction of the Levitical priests and the Levites whom David had organized to be in charge of the house of the Lord... with rejoicing and with singing, <u>according to the order of David</u> (2 Chronicles 23:18).

Josiah became king at eight years old about 641 BC and he also reinstituted Davidic worship (2 Chronicles 34-35).

The singers, the sons of Asaph, were in their place <u>according to the command of David,</u> and Asaph, and Heman, and Jeduthun the king's seer; and the gatekeepers were at each gate. They did not need to depart from their service, for their brothers the Levites prepared for them (2 Chronicles 35:15).

Around 450 BC Ezra and Nehemiah reinstituted Davidic worship after Israel's return from Babylon (Ezra 3:10-11, Nehemiah 12:28–47).

And when the builders laid the foundation of the temple of the Lord, the priests in their vestments came forward with

> *trumpets, and the Levites, the sons of Asaph, with cymbals, to praise the Lord, <u>according to the directions of David</u> king of Israel (Ezra 3:10).*
>
> *And they performed the service of their God and the service of purification, as did the singers and the gatekeepers, <u>according to the command of David</u> and his son Solomon. For long ago in the days of David and Asaph there were directors of the singers, and there were songs of praise and thanksgiving to God (Nehemiah 12:45-46).*

The pattern is clear. The nation's return to the Lord always incorporated a revival of true worship. Repentance for Israel included turning away *from* their sins and idolatry, but it also included a return *to* their original purpose as a kingdom of priests to God. Nearly every king seemed to understand that part of Israel's responsibility was specifically to worship the Lord in the way that David had established during his reign.

It's important to note the timeline of Israel's history. King David ruled Israel around 1000 BC and passed the kingdom off to his son Solomon. Most people believe Amos was written about 250 years later—around 750 BC. Isaiah was likely written close to that same time. It was in this era that God began to prophesy about restoring David's tabernacle (Amos 9:11 and Isaiah 16:5). It would be *after* these prophetic promises from Amos and Isaiah that the kings of Israel would experience spiritual revivals and restore Davidic worship. I point this out because each king would have been aware of these prophecies about David's restored tabernacle, and they chose to reinstate worship according to the order of David. Any notion that God did not want to restore Davidic worship seems to be lost on these faithful kings of Israel. They obviously believed that what David instituted regarding worship was something to be carried on for future generations. They seemed to understand that for them to lead God's people faithfully required His presence at the center of their nation again.

A Covenant and a Kingdom

*I will raise up your offspring after you, one of your own sons,
and I will establish his Kingdom. He shall build a house for me,
and I will establish his throne forever (1 Chronicles 17:11-12).*

The prophesied rebuilding of David's tabernacle in Amos 9:11 includes both the enthronement of Jesus in the heavenly Zion, as well as the restoration of Davidic worship in the church. You cannot ignore either the priestly or the royal fulfillment of God's promise, because God's government flows from a place of worship. While we have already spent much time getting clarity on the power and function of Davidic worship, we need to also clarify the nature of the Kingdom of God—the rule and reign of Jesus Christ on the throne of David.

The Davidic Covenant

The end of 1 Chronicles 16 records that after the launch of David's tabernacle "all the people departed each to his house, and David went home to bless his household." David's home was the palace—he was the king. You can imagine David glancing out the window of his house and seeing the ark in a tent in his backyard. But something in his heart was still not satisfied. David knew that God was the true King of Israel, so it bothered him that he was living in a nicer "house" than God. He called for Nathan the prophet and said:

"Behold, I dwell in a house of cedar, but the ark of the covenant of the Lord is under a tent" (1 Chronicles 17:1).

David wanted to build a permanent house for God's presence. He wanted a true temple established. Since David had a palace, He wanted a palace for Yahweh. The prophet Nathan initially agreed with David's desire to build a permanent temple, but that same night God interrupted Nathan with a prophetic word for the king. This prophecy would become known as the Davidic covenant, and the promises it contains are crucial for us to understand the restoration of David's tabernacle.

First, God promised to establish Israel in a permanent land forever (1 Chronicles 17:7-10). Then God told David that although he wanted to build the Lord a house, instead God would build a house for him (1 Chronicles 17:10). He had determined that David's "offspring" would experience the fulfillment of the desires of David's heart. God promised to establish this offspring as the king of His people as well as the one who would build a "house" for Him (1 Chronicles 17:11-12). David's son Solomon would fulfil a measure of this prophecy, but we now realize Nathan was also prophesying about the coming Messiah. God said He will establish David's offspring on his throne "forever." Clearly Solomon would not reign forever, but one of David's sons would somehow fulfill this prophecy about an everlasting Kingdom.

Interestingly, the only time the phrase "Kingdom of God" is found in the Old Testament is when David refers to his son Solomon's coming reign over Israel (1 Chronicles 28:5). Surely David had his covenant with God in mind when he used this language. Yet he also must have realized that Solomon would only foreshadow the One who would sit on the throne forever. It would take another Son to ultimately fulfill the prophetic word given to David and establish the Kingdom of God on the earth. It was Jesus, called the Son of David throughout the Scriptures, who accomplished this.

The prophet Isaiah echoes the Davidic covenant in its promise of the Son to be born who would become King. We love to quote this passage sentimentally at Christmas time, but this prophetic promise is that the coming child would rule and reign on the throne of David forever with righteousness and justice.

For unto us a Child is born, Unto us a Son is given... Of the increase of his government and of peace there will be no end, on the throne of David and over his Kingdom, to establish it and to uphold it with justice and with righteousness from this time forth and forevermore (Isaiah 9:6-7).

The "throne of David" that Isaiah references speaks to the reign of this Son over God's Kingdom from Jerusalem. In light of promises like these, the Jewish people were literally expecting a human king from David's line who would re-establish the nation of Israel in its land and bring back the "glory days" of David's united reign. They did not realize that the coming Messiah would actually be Yahweh Himself in the flesh—fully God and fully man. God came. The child was born. Fulfilling the Davidic covenant, Jesus came and established His house—the church, the house of prayer, the restored tabernacle of David. His people would become "living stones," built together as a dwelling place of God's presence (1 Peter 2:5, Ephesians 2:22).

God told David "I will build you a house" (1 Chron. 17:10) and Jesus told his disciples "I will build my church" (Matthew 16:18). David's dream would be realized in Christ, as He established a spiritual temple of His presence and glory, not built by human hands (Acts 7:48, 17:24, 2 Cor. 5:1). David wanted to build a place for God in Israel. He wanted God's presence and God's Kingdom to be fully manifest among them. That desire was godly, but it would take Jesus Himself to come and make a way for the manifestation of that desire. After His resurrection, Jesus ascended to the right hand of the Father and sat down on the heavenly throne of David in the heavenly Jerusalem. His reign is forever, thus fulfilling the promise to David that His "offspring" would govern the Kingdom without end.

The Kingdom of God

At this point it could be helpful to clarify what I mean when I refer to the Kingdom of God. The "Kingdom" of God is the reign of God; wherever God is in charge, it is His Kingdom. That is why "Kingdom of God" is synonymous in Scripture with the "kingdom of heaven." Remember that I referred to heaven as God's "man cave." It is where His perfect will is done. And when things on earth align with God's leadership, God's Kingdom is present.

> God told David "I will build you a house" and Jesus told his disciples "I will build my church." David's dream would be realized in Christ, as He established a spiritual temple of His presence and glory, not built by human hands

Therefore, it is impossible to be disobedient towards God and be part of His Kingdom. Since Adam and Eve sinned, humanity has been in rebellion to God and the earth itself has been in turmoil. The apostle Paul says that earth "groans" because of the brokenness of sin (Romans 8). Yet because of the death, resurrection, and ascension of Jesus, the Kingdom of God is now accessible. When a person follows Jesus and becomes a Christian, they enter into God's Kingdom. They come under the leadership of Christ and accept Him as their Lord and King.

Jesus compares the Kingdom of God to leaven in dough (Matthew 13:33). It gradually works its way through the entire lump. Likewise, the Kingdom of God is advancing on the earth through the church. Jesus did not come initially to establish His political reign on the earth as many expected. Instead, He dropped the seed of God's Kingdom into the hearts of His followers and is allowing it to spread throughout the globe. As God's people influence the earth, the Kingdom moves forward.

As the church walks in power, preaching the gospel, leading people to Jesus, casting out demons, healing the sick, making disciples and transforming culture, we are manifesting God's Kingdom on the earth. Jesus said when you see demonic spirits come under His subjection, you know that the Kingdom of God is near (Luke 11:20). The advancement of God's Kingdom is described as "violence" (Matthew 11:12) and a "shaking" of the earth (Hebrews 12:25-29). For God to rule over a person or a place, it means anything in contradiction to Him must be confronted.

That confrontation will escalate into the ultimate conflict at the end of the age. God's Kingdom will fully manifest at the return of Jesus to the earth. At that point, all evil and sin will be destroyed and God will have his way completely. Jesus will make all things new (Revelation 21:5). The One who sits on the throne of David in the heavenly Jerusalem is coming again to manifest His Kingdom on the earth in totality.

Therefore, God's Kingdom is both "now" and "not yet."[1]

---

1   The idea that God's Kingdom is "already but not yet" was popularized by George Eldon Ladd. See, for instance, his book *The Gospel of the Kingdom*.

God's Kingdom is coming when Jesus returns, but it's also here now, in a measure, through the church. People and places are coming under God's leadership every day, but many will resist His authority until He comes in the flesh and forces His dominion with power. Some try to focus on one or the other—Kingdom now or not yet—and they miss the fullness of what the Bible describes. It's both.

A Global Restoration

With this in mind, we can expect a measure of the restoration of David's tabernacle in this age, and its fullness in the age to come. Whatever God is (re)building and restoring is eschatological — in other words, it is connected to the end times, when God will culminate His redemptive purposes. However, because of His mercy and grace, He has given us the church age to experience now a foretaste of the age to come. The restoration of David's tabernacle is not only a future promise, but a present reality. Heaven is not just something we wait for but something we actively seek. Jesus told us to seek first the Kingdom of God (Matthew 6:33).

My understanding of the biblical perspective on the end times is that the contrast between good and evil will increase as we near Jesus's return (Isaiah 60:2). The light will get brighter as the darkness gets darker. I believe we should expect to see increasing global persecution, tribulation, and martyrdom of the church. But I also believe we should expect to see great revival, signs and wonders, and a great harvest of souls happening simultaneously with the trouble. The prophet Joel promises a great outpouring of God's Spirit at the end of the age. He describes those days as both the "great" and "terrible" day of the Lord (Joel 2:28-31). Jesus describes global turmoil but also promises that the gospel will be preached to every people group before His return (Matthew

24:14). All these things will be happening at the same time as the nations' rage against Jesus and His impending Kingdom (Psalm 2:1-3).

Because David's restored tabernacle includes both Davidic worship and the Kingdom of God, we should expect to see a global increase in Davidic worship as we near the return of Christ and the Kingdom continues to expand. Isaiah specifically prophesied of an explosion of praise and worship around the world before the Messiah comes to judge the earth (Isaiah 42:10-13). Malachi 1:11 also describes a global "incense" of worship and prayer in "every place." We have yet to see this fully manifested, but it is coming. In fact, I believe the expansion of God's Kingdom and the promised great harvest of souls are connected to the establishment of Davidic worship on the earth.

If God is truly enthroned in praises, then those praises must precede the advancement of the Kingdom. If heaven is not just the place of God's reign but the place of day and night worship and intercession, then the increasing Kingdom of heaven must include expressions of heavenly worship and prayer.

> As the church walks in power, preaching the gospel, leading people to Jesus, casting out demons, healing the sick, making disciples and transforming culture, we are manifesting God's kingdom on the earth.

"The largest global harvest in history will come directly on the heels of the extravagant sound of love, adoration and praise that is released... We are going to witness first hand the beautiful

147

correlation between the fire ignited in our hearts and the release of the fragrance and aroma of Christ on the Earth."[2]

Just as David's tabernacle made way for Solomon's temple, the worshiping church is making way for the age to come. You will remember that Solomon continued the Davidic worship established by his father. In fact, David provided the land, supplies, funding, and manpower for the temple that his son built (see 1 Chronicles 22). By the time David passed off the Kingdom to Solomon, he had 4,000 trained musicians and had raised the equivalent of billions of dollars to fund the project. Rather than a stark shift from David to Solomon, you see a season of preparation leading up to a time of culmination. David's tabernacle didn't end with Solomon's temple. The tent essentially merged into the temple. I believe this paints a picture of what we can expect as we near the Lord's return. Even amid global calamity and tribulation, there will be pockets of heaven on earth before Jesus comes back. I don't know what it will look like, but I believe our Kingdom efforts in this age will converge with the age to come, just as David's tabernacle shifted into Solomon's temple. What we do now matters immensely for eternity.

The context of Amos's prophecy of David's tabernacle includes a promise of a time when the "the plowman shall overtake the reaper" and "the mountains shall drip sweet wine" (Amos 9:13). The plowman overtaking the reaper represents a rapid harvest of souls coming into the Kingdom and the wine represents the outpouring of God's Spirit with power, healing, signs, wonders, and miracles. As the global prayer and worship movement increases across the world, God has promised the manifestation of His supernatural power, as well as a great

---

2   Sean Feucht and Andy Byrd, *Fire and Fragrance: From the Great Commandment to the Great Commission* (Shippensburg, PA: Destiny Image), 32.

missions movement where millions of people will come to the Lord throughout the nations of the earth.

David's tabernacle is being restored. It began with the ascension of Jesus to the throne of David in heaven, and it is perpetuated by the enthronement of God upon the praises of His people through Davidic worship. As heaven is reflected on earth through day and night worship and prayer, God's presence is manifested. As God dwells among His worshiping, praying, priestly church, the Kingdom of God increases globally. This restoration will climax with the return of Jesus, at which point He will literally rule and reign on the earth. At that point, the tabernacle of God will be with men, God will restore all things and we will enter fully into our eternal calling as priests and kings in the new heavens and new earth (Revelation 21:3). The original dream of Eden in God's heart and the vision of a resting place in David's heart will finally be realized.

> **David's tabernacle is being restored. It began with the ascension of Jesus to the throne of David in heaven, and it is perpetuated by the enthronement of God upon the praises of His people through Davidic worship.**

Even now, we are experiencing a restoration of David's tabernacle. Davidic worship is increasing. God's Kingdom is advancing. And we have a unique opportunity in this age to invite the nations into the "tent" to experience God's presence and enter God's Kingdom.

The Rest of Mankind

I will return and will rebuild the tabernacle of David... So that the rest of mankind may seek the Lord (Acts 15:16-17).

I have spent nearly twenty years in leadership of various expressions of Davidic worship, and have experienced firsthand the connection between worship in the spirit of the tabernacle of David and the transformative impact on individual lives, as well as on cities and nations. When believers come together to host the presence of God with day-and-night, prophetic worship and prayer, it propels the advance of the kingdom of God in a region. I could give several examples of how this has played out in our ministry experience, but an example involving a literal tent seems most fitting.

Worship Helps Transform Lives

There's something about a tent in particular that gives us a beautiful image of God's heart for the lost to come back home to Him. A tent is open and inviting—a vivid demonstration of the invitation found in the gospel of Christ. My journey of participating in tent gatherings began when we started to build relationships with similar prayer groups around North Carolina. In 2013, I was busy leading the Boiler Room when God told me to begin to reach out to leaders of similar ministries in our state and region. God also spoke to me about David Bradshaw, who was organizing an effort in Virginia to connect prayer and worship groups there in partnership with one another (I'll come back to David in a minute).

One of the leaders I met in that season was Mike Thornton, who lived in Wilmington, NC. He was writing a book on revival history in eastern North Carolina and was feeling stirred about hosting tent revival gatherings. We brought our ministry efforts together in 2014 to host our first tent gathering that featured day and night worship and prayer in Dunn, NC. Dunn was a significant location during the Azusa Street revival of the early 1900s. The tent was dubbed "The Jesus Tent" and we partnered with Mike to host several tent gatherings from 2014 to 2017— primarily in eastern North Carolina. Each gathering featured day and night worship, prayer, and outreach. God moved powerfully every time! I could take a whole chapter to tell stories, but I want to highlight one.

We finally brought the Jesus Tent to our hometown in Greenville, NC in 2016. We hosted 100 hours of non-stop worship, gave away free meals, and ministered to the surrounding low-income neighborhood. One of our first nights, a young couple came from across the street to get free hot dogs at the tent. Someone from our ministry team started talking to them and quickly led them to the Lord. This couple lived in a house across the street from the tent.

The next day the outreach team visited their house, where they found a great-grandmother in her wheelchair. Multiple generations of her family lived in the same small house with her. The team discovered that she was a praying believer who was longing for her family to be saved. She had been crying out to God for years. It turned out that ten or twelve people were home at that point, and they were invited into the room. After our team shared the gospel with them, the whole family got on their knees and accepted Christ! Years of sowing in prayer led to a bountiful harvest that day!

A few days later, they brought grandma over to the tent to enjoy the worship. While she was there, a local newspaper came to do a report on the tent gathering. They ended up talking to her and others from her household, and their story became front page news. The family shared how the culture of their home had shifted, and they were no longer arguing with each other since turning to Jesus. The front page had a photo of this grandma smiling in the tent with the headline: WORSHIP HELPS TRANSFORM LIVES.

This is the power of the presence of God. When we began to host God's presence with day and night worship and prayer in that neighborhood, the prayers of grandma were answered—God's kingdom was manifested dramatically and lives were changed forever. This amazing testimony reminds me of the story when Paul and Silas had been flogged and thrown into jail. As they sang hymns and prayed at midnight, God sent an earthquake that broke them free from their shackles. They were able to share the Gospel with the jailer and his entire household began to follow Jesus (Acts 16:25-34).

Tents are a Silver Bullet

There is something about tents that speaks so profoundly to God's desire to invite people who don't yet know Him to experience His presence. On a practical level, tents of day and night worship create an easy environment for the body of Christ to come together in unity, without gathering in one particular church building. They also provide an easy way for the general public to wander in and experience God's presence. Since a tent is not a formal church building, there is much less pressure. Not only do tents point prophetically to the deeper truths of David's Tabernacle, but they serve practically in our modern times to manifest the spirit of the tabernacle of David in public places. Interestingly, North Carolina's Jesus Tent is not the only day and night worship tent that has surfaced in recent years.

About a year before the Jesus Tent was set up in our home state, a group of YWAM missionaries hosted forty days of non-stop worship on the National Mall in Washington DC. After hosting David's Tent DC as a special event for two more years, they decided to launch into a 24/7/365 schedule on September 11, 2015, and the worship has not stopped since! This perpetual love song to Jesus is the only modern expression of continual worship that I'm aware of that takes place under a literal tent.

A few years after David's Tent DC began their unceasing expression of worship, God began to stir another group about tents. David Bradshaw, who I mentioned earlier, was leading a house of prayer in Fredericksburg, Virginia as well as helping to unite prayer groups across their state. God brought up David Bradshaw's name to me when He began speaking to me about unity among prayer groups. In 2017, David and Jason Hershey, the founder of David's Tent DC, received a vision from God to host fifty tents on the National Mall in Washington DC with simultaneous day and night worship. The idea was that each state in the nation would host a tent with worshipers from their state filling the hours.

This dream became a reality in October of 2017. Over 1,000 worship teams helped host three days of day and night worship, prayer, and outreach for the first national Awaken the Dawn gathering. Tens of thousands of worshipers converged in America's capital for a historic gathering. Not only was it an amazing expression of unity, but God's presence was palpable throughout the event. As the country came together to host God in their capital city, dozens of unbelievers got saved, many were healed, and the crime even slowed down across Washington DC during that time. Now Awaken the Dawn has grown into an ongoing movement centered on uniting the church to host God's presence through day and night worship, prayer, and outreach. Tents are set up every year (sometimes hundreds at a time), and God moves powerfully through these public expressions of Jesus's worth.

I believe this increase in tent gatherings is God speaking to His church about the importance of understanding David's tabernacle. I also believe God has been inviting those in the global prayer movement to take the presence of God into the streets, parks, campuses, and public places to see God's life-changing presence crash into a lost and broken world. If God's presence changes everything, then we must not keep it to ourselves.

The Tent is Open

This era of history, between the first and second comings of Jesus to the earth, provide a unique time for the nations to enter a covenant relationship with God. David's tabernacle gives us a vivid picture of this truth. Just as David's tent had no veil and was open for the Gentiles to engage in worship, Jesus has opened the door for anyone to come into God's presence through faith in Him. David's tabernacle symbolizes a time when the Gentiles (the nations) can enter into our original purpose as worshippers of Yahweh.

You will remember that during David's reign there were two tents. One was Moses's tabernacle that remained in Gibeon, with all the ornate furniture, animal sacrifices, and Old Covenant rituals. The priests continued to follow the Law, but there was one thing missing—the ark of the covenant. They were going through the motions of worship without the presence of God. The other tent was David's tabernacle. It was in Jerusalem with the ark. There the Levites offered sacrifices of praise from their hearts before the Lord. Their worship in Zion was centered on God's presence. They were interacting directly with the Lord in a real relationship.

These two tents point to the two options we are given in this age. Jesus has established a New Covenant with His people by shedding His blood on the cross. As Jesus's body was torn, the veil of the Jerusalem temple was also torn. God has made a way for relationships with His people again. David's tabernacle points us to this New Covenant reality where there is no veil of separation between us and God—where we can come boldly to His throne of grace. The "ark" of God's presence is accessible to Christians because of the work of Christ.

The tent in Gibeon is the tent of empty religion. There the rituals continued without the presence of God, just as many church-goers go through the motions of Christianity while detached from true intimacy with the Lord. Jesus warned of those who honor Him with their lips while their hearts are far from Him (Matthew 15:8). This kind of religiosity tries to earn with our piety what Jesus has purchased for us and offers us freely. There are still two "tabernacles" operating at the same time in our day. The tabernacle of self-righteousness and the tabernacle of grace. The tent of Moses and the tent of David.

This unique time in history is not only our opportunity to enjoy an intimate relationship with God through Christ, but it is our opportunity to invite others into relationship with God too. In the book of Acts, we find a final reference to the tabernacle of David in Scripture, and it is connected to this very idea that the nations are invited into the presence of God.

In Acts 15, the apostle James quotes Amos 9:11 at a pivotal moment for the early church. Christianity had begun in Jerusalem at Pentecost, but persecution had caused Christians to disperse into the surrounding regions. As they went, they naturally shared the gospel (Acts 11:19). The city of Antioch became a major hub for Christian activity at that time, and it began to create quite a stir. Barnabas went from Jerusalem to check out what God was doing and led Saul (later called Paul) there as well. From Antioch, Paul and Barnabas were sent out as the first Christian missionaries, and the gospel expanded to new cities and regions.

The multi-ethnic expansion of Christianity became a topic of debate among Christian leaders who were primarily Jewish. How "jewish" would they require the new Gentiles converts to become? Would they need to be circumcised, for instance? Debates about these issues led to the Jerusalem council in Acts 15. At this council, after a time of sharing testimonies and discussion, James stood up to quote Amos 9:11 to the apostles and church leaders.

"'After this I will return and will rebuild the tabernacle of David, which has fallen down; I will rebuild its ruins, and I will set it up; So that the rest of mankind may seek the Lord, Even all the Gentiles who are called by My name,' says the Lord who does all these things" (Acts 15:16-17, NKJV).

James tweaked some of the language of Amos to fit the given context. He said that God was rebuilding the tabernacle of David for a specific purpose: "so that the rest of mankind may seek the Lord." He realized that God's plan all along was to reach "the rest of mankind" with the gospel and David's tabernacle was part of that plan.

After the debate, the church leaders at the Jerusalem council agreed to allow the Gentiles to be Christians without being circumcised or becoming overly "jewish." The apostles used an interesting phrase when they communicated their decision to the church. They said, "For it seemed good to the Holy Spirit and to us..." (Acts 15:28). I was familiar with this phrase, so it stuck out to me when I was rereading the story of David's tabernacle. Notice that King David said, "If it seems good to you, and if it is of the Lord our God..." (1 Chronicles 13:2) when he was proposing that they bring the ark of the covenant into Jerusalem. The apostles were sitting in Jerusalem, James was quoting a prophecy about David's tabernacle, and then they used nearly identical terminology that David used when he established his original tabernacle. David said, "If it seems good to you, and if it is of the Lord our God." The apostles said,

> This unique time in history is not only our opportunity to enjoy an intimate relationship with God through Christ, but it is our opportunity to invite others into relationship with God too.

"For it seemed good to the Holy Spirit and to us." David said this while establishing a revolutionary way for people (even Gentiles) to experience God's presence. The apostles said this while embracing a revolutionary way for people (even Gentiles) to experience God's presence in Christ Jesus! I personally have not found any other instance in Scripture with similar phrasing. The similarities seem more than a coincidence.

Worship and Missions

The need for a council was sparked by what was happening at the church in Antioch, and there are a few things worth noting about this important Christian hub. The believers there were ministering to the Lord, fasting, and praying. These new Christians had grasped their calling to function as a priesthood before the Lord. In fact, there was something suspiciously *Davidic* about what was happening there.

> As they ministered to the Lord and fasted, the Holy Spirit said, "Now separate to Me Barnabas and Saul for the work to which I have called them." Then, having fasted and prayed, and laid hands on them, they sent them away (Acts 13:2-3).

This context and culture of worship and prayer is the environment from which God would send forth Saul (Paul) into his initial missionary journey.[1] This would become Paul's missions base from which he would embark on all his church planting and apostolic ministry. This was the first time we see any believers intentionally engaging in fasting or cross-cultural outreach. Prior to this, the Christians in Jerusalem ministered locally. Before Antioch, the only time the gospel began to spread outside of their immediate context was when persecution began to force the believers to be dispersed from Jerusalem. The fact that any non-Jews are Christians today is largely due to the pioneering missions ministry that flowed out of Antioch. It is no coincidence that this congregation's primary activity seems to be ministering to God in worship, and that it is also the first place from which missionaries were sent. I believe it's likely that Antioch was the first church that really began to manifest God's desire for Christians to engage in Davidic worship. Like the Morvians in Herrnhut, the church at Antioch's intense focus on devotion to the Lord began to launch them into the Great Commission to make disciples of all the nations (Matthew 28:19-20).

Another "Davidic" facet to the community at Antioch was

---

1   Interestingly, Paul's first recorded sermon after he leaves Antioch is centered on David. King David is mentioned four times in Acts 13.

their ethnic diversity. When you study the Antioch leadership team, listed in Acts 13:1, you find a multi-ethnic group of teachers and prophets working together in unity. Just as David's tabernacle extended an invitation to some Gentiles to participate in the priesthood, Antioch was extending the bounds of what was acceptable in Christian worship, leadership, and mission.

There are hints at this international dimension to David's tabernacle in the original story. I have already mentioned how Obed-Edom, the Gentile who temporarily housed the ark of the covenant, was invited to serve at the tabernacle as a gatekeeper. You will also notice another foreshadowing in the very first song sung at David's tent. The first prophetic song ever sung on Mount Zion was an invitation to the nations to come worship God.

Sing to the Lord, all the earth; Proclaim the good news of His salvation from day to day. Declare His glory among the nations, His wonders among all peoples (I Chronicles 16:24).

The idea that God was inviting all people groups into relationship with Him was instilled at the very foundation of the Davidic order of worship. What David established for Israel was always meant to be expanded to the nations of the earth. As we have seen, it took Jesus to begin to manifest the global aspect of David's tabernacle that was always in God's heart.

John Piper articulates this convergence of worship and missions perfectly when he says that worship is the fuel and goal of missions.[2] Reaching people far from God with the gospel and

---

2   "Worship... is the fuel and goal of missions. it's the goal of missions because in missions we simply aim to bring the Nations into the white hot enjoyment of God's glory.... But worship is also the fuel of missions. Passion for God and worship proceeds the offer of God in preaching. You can't commend what you don't cherish... missions begins and ends in worship." John Piper, *Let the Nations Be Glad*, 2nd ed. (Grand Rapids, MI: Baker Academic, 1993, 2003), 17.

seeing them restored to God in Christ must include them becoming passionate worshipers. I have already made a strong case that worship is God's original purpose for humanity. If that is the case, then worship is certainly the goal of missions. Worship is also the fuel, because we naturally invite others to enjoy what we enjoy! If Jesus is our supreme delight and treasure, then we will speak of Him to others. The biblical pattern that we see so vividly with the story of Antioch is that worshipers who love God will go and invite others to worship Him. Those new worshipers will then invite others to join too. So worship becomes the fuel and goal of missions.

> The idea that God was inviting all people groups into relationship with Him was instilled at the very foundation of the Davidic order of worship. What David established for Israel was always meant to be expanded to the nations of the earth.

Believers worshiping under a tent is a beautiful picture of this reality. It's as simple as worshipers inviting others to come join them under the canopy of God's presence: "Come see what I see. Come feel what I feel. Come experience what I'm experiencing. Come and worship Jesus with me."

This is what the rebuilding of David's tabernacle is all about, and it is this glorious truth that launched me years ago from my summer camp experience into my ministry. I had encountered God's presence and wanted others to experience His life-changing presence too.

Conclusion

Throughout this book, we have journeyed along three parallel paths that expound on my original premise: that God's presence changes everything.

First, I have shared personal stories and testimonies from my life and ministry journey that attest to what happens when we prioritize God's presence through prophetic worship and prayer: lives, families, and cities are transformed.

Second, and more importantly, we've journeyed through the witness of Scripture and seen that God's original purpose for mankind is to be a royal priesthood that worships the Lord and stewards the earth as a temple of His glory forever. King David's reign in Jerusalem, and the tabernacle he established, stand as a blueprint of community that hosts the presence of God and ministers to Him day and night. This heavenly pattern of worship that David pioneered is emerging again in our day.

This leads us to the third path we explored: the journey of Jesus. In nearly every chapter, I have pointed to Christ and the gospel of the Kingdom. What He has done, and what He is going to do, will not only restore and fulfill the longing David had for a dwelling place for God on the earth, but will also accomplish all that God originally intended in His heart for mankind.

Jesus is rebuilding David's tabernacle. He has come to us, and

He is coming again. Even now, across the nations, He is taking His place at the center of His church, and He will rule and reign on the throne of David forever.

May we learn to prioritize the presence of Jesus in our lives, homes, churches, and cities. May we minister to Him day and night with prophetic songs and intercessory prayers. May we take the good news to the ends of the earth, so that every tribe and tongue will sing a new song to the Lamb of God who is worthy of it all.

Select Bibliography

Barnes, Albert. "Psalms 134" in *Albert Barnes' Notes on the Whole Bible*. Posted on *Studylight.org*. https://www.studylight. org/commentaries/eng/bnb/psalms-134.html.

Beale, G.K. *The Temple and the Church's Mission: A Biblical Theology of the Dwelling Place of God*. Madison, Wisconsin: InterVarsity Press Academic, 2004.

Bickle, Mike. *Growing in Prayer: A Real-Life Guide to Talking with God*. Lake Mary, FL: Charisma House, 2014.

Burns, Chris. *Pioneers of His Presence*. Self-published, 2014.

Conner, Kevin. *The Tabernacle of David*. Portland, OR: City Bible Publishing, 1976.

Dickson, John and Pierce, Chuck D. *Worship As It Is In Heaven*. Ventura, CA: Gospel Light, 2010.

Eastman, Dick. *Intercessory Worship: Combining Worship & Prayer to Touch the Heart of God*. Grand Rapids, MI: Chosen Books, 2011.

Everett, Stephen. *The Sound That Changed Everything*. Shippensburg, PA: Treasure House, an imprint of Destiny Image, 2003.

Fritch, David. *Enthroned: Bringing God's Kingdom to Earth Through Unceasing Worship & Prayer*. Independently published, 2017.

Greig, Pete. *How to Pray: A Simple Guide for Normal People*. Colorado Springs, CO: Navpress, 2019.

Greig, Pete and Roberts, Dave. *Red Moon Rising: Rediscover the Power of Prayer*. Colorado Springs, CO: Navpress, 2015.

Hahn, Scott W. *The Kingdom of God as Liturgical Empire*. Grand Rapids, MI: Baker Academic, 2012.

Hayford, Jack. *The Reward of Worship: The Joy of Fellowship with a Personal God*. Grand Rapids, MI: Chosen Books, 2005.

The Harmony of the Divine Dispensations. Public domain. https://play.google.com/store/books/details?id=IjxVAAAAcAAJ

Herbert, A.G. *The Throne of David*. 7th impression. London: Faber and Faber Limited, 1956.

Henry, Matthew. "Leviticus 6," in *Matthew Henry's Commentary on the Whole Bible*. Posted on Bible Hub. https://biblehub.com/commentaries/mhcw/leviticus/6.htm.

Humphrey, Billy. *Unceasing*. 2nd ed. Kansas City, MO: Forerunner Publishing, 2009, 2015.

Josephus. *Antiquities of the Jews*. Public domain.

Joyner, Rick. *The World Aflame: The Welsch Revival and Its Lessons For Our Time*. Charlotte, NC: Morningstar Publications, 1993.

Kleinig, John W. *The Lord's Song*. Sheffield, England: Sheffield Academic Press, 1993.

Layzell, Reginald. *Pastor's Pen: Firsthand Accounts of the 1948 Prophetic Revival*. Independently published, 2019.

Leithart, Peter J. *From Silence to Song: The Davidic Liturgical Revolution*. Moscow, ID: Canon Press, 2003.

———. *1 & 2 Chronicles*. Grand Rapids, MI: Brazos Press, 2019.

Lewis, C.S. *Reflections on the Psalms*. Edison, NJ: First Inspirational Press, 1994.

The Memorial Days of the Renewed Church of the Brethren. 1895. https://www.moravianarchives.org/wp-content/uploads/2012/01/Memorial-Days-b.pdf

Piper, John. *Let the Nations Be Glad*. 2nd ed. Grand Rapids, MI: Baker Academic, 1993, 2003.

The Strongest Strong's Exhaustive Concordance of the Bible. Grand Rapids, MI: Zondervan, 2001.

Tozer, A.W. *The Knowledge of the Holy*. New York, NY: HarperCollins, 1961.

About the Author

Matthew Lilley is an author, worship leader, intercessor, and Bible teacher with a passion for God's presence, extravagant worship and prayer, and a desire to see cities transformed by Jesus. He has helped launch two houses of prayer in North Carolina and has also served in national leadership roles with worship and prayer movements such as Burn 24-7 and Awaken the Dawn. In 2004 he founded Presence Pioneers to help fulfill his calling to connect, equip, and plant presence-centered Christian communities. You can connect with Matthew at his personal website: www.presencepioneer.com

Presence Pioneers is a Christian nonprofit organization that has helped inspire, launch, and lead multiple expressions of worship & prayer ministry since being founded in 2004 by Matthew Lilley. Throughout its history, the organization has carried the spirit of the Tabernacle of David—a passion for God's presence, extravagant worship & prayer, and a desire to see cities transformed by Jesus.

Vision: To build day-and-night worship & prayer for regional revival that touches the nations with the Gospel of Jesus Christ

Mission: To connect, equip, and plant presence-centered worship & prayer communities

You can learn more at presencepioneers.org

A weekly leadership podcast that helps you and your community host the presence of God through day & night worship & prayer—because we believe God's presence changes everything. Episodes feature short Bible teachings or extended interviews with key leaders in the prayer & worship movement where we discuss topics such as prophetic worship, intercessory prayer, global missions, unity in the Church, revival, and David's tabernacle.

Available on Apple Podcasts, Spotify, Google Podcasts, Youtube and anywhere you listen to podcasts.

LEADERSHIP NETWORK

The ATD Nationwide Leadership Network is a decentralized, relational family of leaders with a shared value of hosting the presence of God through day and night worship, prayer and missions. The network includes leaders who are stewarding expressions of worship & prayer across America who want to connect with other like-minded leaders. We each serve within our own ministries, cities and campuses while also coming together collectively for relational connection and strategic initiatives suchas Tent America.

Our vision is to see a family of presence-centered communities in every state and region, walking in John 17 unity and collectively worshiping and praying day & night for a Great Awakening in America and the nations. We want to disciple America in hosting the presence of God together.

Sign up at awakenthedawn.com/leadership-network/ or scan the QR code below with your phone's camera